# LAUGH WITH THE JUDGE

# LAUGH WITH THE JUDGE

## Humorous Anecdotes from a Career on the Bench

by Bruce Littlejohn
Associate Justice,
The Supreme Court
of South Carolina

The Sandlapper Store, Inc.
1974

LIBRARY OF CONGRESS CATALOG CARD NUMBER: 74-22868

FIRST EDITION



INTERNATIONAL STANDARD BOOK NUMBER: 0-87844-025-9

*Published by*

THE SANDLAPPER STORE, INC.
P. O. BOX 841, LEXINGTON, S. C. 29072

MANUFACTURED IN THE UNITED STATES OF AMERICA

*To the Memory*

*of*

My Mother and Father

*Who Gave Me Opportunity*

# MIRTH FROM THE MAINSTREAM

From the pen of a native and noted South Carolina jurist who long was a co-maker of laws in the State Legislature and subsequently became charged with duties as a Circuit Judge and State Supreme Court Justice, comes this harvest of homespun humor, *Laugh With The Judge.* Here, uniquely and refreshingly different among new books is a delightful levity leavening of the legal loaf, presented in varied and fascinating format.

No fantasy or fiction is within its pages. This assembly of authentic anecdotes consists entirely of actual incidents in which real people move into amusing animation from the author's rich reminiscences, gleaned during his many years at the bar, in the legislative halls, the political arena and on the bench, with some recollections from his World War II Army life in the United States and overseas. They are the product of his congenial all-levels liaison with people in every walk of life, chiefly in South Carolina, where his friends are legion.

The author, State Supreme Court Justice Cameron Bruce Littlejohn, has written sans satire, safeguarding long-established court decorum, and with his characteristic warm humanism. The total tone of the tome is candidly personal but in friendly vein. The abundant round-up of humorous incidents involves judges, jurors, attorneys, defendants, politicians, bailiffs and other court attachés, servicemen, prominent people, just plain folks and a wide variety of others with whom he has had personal contact since the late and beloved Dr. Henry Nelson Snyder handed him his degree at Wofford College in 1935.

Justice Littlejohn is well qualified by personal experience to write about the men and women he has had contact with in virtually every layer of the social strata. He has a genuine fondness for people and is endowed with a keen sense of humor and an in-depth understanding of the moods and mysteries of human behavior.

Long ago another author wrote, "Memory is the treasure house of the mind." Into this volume, Justice Littlejohn has opened a large section of the storehouse of his recollections, thereby creating a valuable contribution to Palmetto State factual literature and extending his skill as an excellent and entertaining storyteller. We will not digress to touch upon any one anecdote or group of stories. Our rating for the whole is superb.

Civic club program chairmen and political stump speakings' masters of ceremonies often cut short their introductions of locally or area well-known speakers simply by saying, "This man needs no introduction." We readily realize that Bruce Littlejohn doesn't either, except to newcomers to South Carolina or other readers who have kept close to their homes and away from courthouses and mixings into politics, but "just for the record":

Justice Littlejohn was born July 22, 1913, at Pacolet, a son of Cameron and Lady Sara (Warmoth) Littlejohn. He graduated from Wofford College with an A.B. degree in 1935, and from the University of South Carolina Law School, where he was President of the Senior Law Class, with an LL.B. degree in 1936. In 1968 Wofford conferred upon him the degree LL.D., and in 1970 the University of South Carolina conferred upon him the degree J.D. He married Inell Smith of Inman on February 7, 1942. She passed away on July 16, 1962. Two children were born to the marriage: Inell Smith Littlejohn (now Mrs. Dan L. Allen, III), and Cameron Bruce Littlejohn, Jr., who is a law student at the University of South Carolina.

Justice Littlejohn is a member of Blue Key, Spartanburg Civitan Club, the American Legion, 40 and 8, Veterans of Foreign Wars and the First Baptist Church of Spartanburg. A veteran of World War II, Pacific Theatre of Operations, he resigned as a member of the South Carolina House of Representatives on October 25, 1943, to volunteer into the Armed Forces and was discharged as a first lieutenant after foreign service, including an assignment as a Japanese war criminals prosecutor in the Philippines. His many services have included duties as a delegate to several county and state and two national Democratic conventions, member of the Judicial Council (chairman of its Committee on Judicial Procedure and Congested Dockets, 1957-67), delegate to the National Conference of State Trial Judges, 1964-66, and delegate to the National Appellate Judges Conference, 1967-73. He is a permanent member of the Fourth United States Circuit Court of Appeals Judicial Conference. His other services have included membership on the National and Schools Awards Jury of Freedoms Foundation at Valley Forge, 1968; the Editorial Committee of the Trial Judges Journal, 1965-67; the Board of Trustees, North Greenville Junior College, 1962-67; and the Wofford College Alumni Board of Directors, 1966-68.

He also served as a member of the State House of Representatives from 1937 to 1943, and from 1947 to 1949 (Speaker 1947-49). He resigned as House member and as Speaker to assume the duties of the office of Judge of the Seventh South Carolina Judicial Circuit, to which he was elected February 9, 1949. His work as circuit judge continued until he was elected an Associate Justice of the South Carolina Supreme Court on January 25, 1967. His home and office are in Spartanburg.

GLEN and SUSAN NAVES
*Retired Newspaper Writers*

Asheville, N. C.
November 1974

# CONTENTS

# WHY THIS BOOK

When the members of the General Assembly of South Carolina elected me Resident Judge of the Seventh Judicial Circuit in 1949, I decided to keep a memorandum of some of the amusing and unusual incidents happening in court, with it in mind to share the experiences with friends and especially with those who elected me. Over the years I kept in my briefcase a small notebook, in which I recorded just enough of the incidents to refresh my memory.

My work as a trial judge (1949 to 1967) required me to hold courts of general sessions (criminal) and common pleas (civil) in all forty-six South Carolina counties. Under our system of rotating circuit judges, each is assigned so that over a period of seven or eight years a judge covers the entire state. Accordingly, I held a series of courts in all counties on two occasions, and three times in most of them.

Some of the anecdotes may resemble humorous happenings previously published, but I have endeavored to record only original occurrences and to refrain from printing any story published heretofore. Many of the names used herein are actually those of the people and places involved. In some instances, however, names have been changed to avoid possible embarrassment.

Most of the incidents related grew out of my work as a trial judge. At the same time, a number of them recall a wider variety of experiences extending back to my academic college days at Wofford College and my law school days at the University of South Carolina. There are included political incidents growing out of my service in the House of Representatives, as Speaker, my work with the Supreme Court of South Carolina since 1967, and a few experiences during my Army service in World War II.

*Laugh With The Judge* is not a "joke book" and was never intended to be. It is a true-to-life chronology of comedy contrasted with the essentially dignified decorum of court proceedings. Understandably, most of the anecdotes will probably be of more interest to judges, lawyers, court attachés and public officeholders, but at the same time it is hoped that many of them will be entertaining to others.

It was originally my plan to reduce the stories to writing and mimeograph them for distribution to the members of the General Assembly who elected me circuit judge in 1949, and to those who elected me to the Supreme Court in 1967, and by so doing to share my experiences with those who made it possible for me to have them. Subsequently it occurred to me that these reminiscences, representing as they do a lighter vein, might be of interest to a broader section of the people. Accordingly, I decided to publish them in book form.

The courtroom is no place for levity. Litigants have vital interests at stake—property rights, freedom, custody of children, etc. A judge is seldom, if ever, justified in precipitating a humorous situation in court. He must not permit improper conduct. At the same time, the law of averages dictates that in the processing of thousands of cases humorous situations will occur, just as funny things will happen in church and even occasionally at a funeral. After these courtroom incidents occur, there is no reason why they should not be recorded and shared.

* * *

I acknowledge my indebtedness:

To my departed friend L. A. Odom, for his encouragement to write and publish this book; to Susan and Glen Naves, retired newspaper writers, for their editing and suggestions; to my secretary, Mrs. Mae King, for her many hours of skilled typing, editing and suggestions; and to my son, Cameron Bruce Littlejohn, Jr., for his review of the manuscript and innumerable recommendations.

BRUCE LITTLEJOHN

# I APPROACH THE BENCH

## *Legal Learning Lost*

Soon after I was elected Seventh Judicial Circuit Judge, I met an old friend on Main Street in Spartanburg and learned he was considerably mixed up concerning the work I had been elected to perform.

It is interesting to note that he had never sought my services when I was a practicing attorney. Obviously he had learned that I had become a judge and he had the impression that in addition to being on the bench I could also continue to practice law. So he proposed to call on me at my office, saying he had a case he wanted me to handle.

I told him I would not be able to accept his case because I no longer was practicing law.

"Judge, don't you practice any law whatsoever?" he inquired, apparently skeptical concerning what I had just told him.

I repeated, "No, I do not practice law," and explained, "I not only am not permitted to practice, but in addition I don't have the time if it were permitted."

Still puzzled, he asked, "Well, didn't you go to law school?"

I answered, "Yes, sir, I did study at the law school."

Sympathetically, he said, "Ain't that a pity? Now, you don't need it and can't use it."

## *Bench Birthing Pains*

A newly elected judge holds his first court with considerable apprehension.

He worries that he may make a slip or some unintentional departure from decorum during his debut on the bench, causing embarrassment to himself or others.

Some uneasiness in this respect accompanied me when I went to Aiken to conduct my first session as circuit judge in January 1950.

My daughter Inell was about three at the time. When I bade her goodbye on Sunday and headed out, she asked me where I was going and I told her my destination was Aiken Courthouse.

While I was away, one of my friends inquired of her where her daddy was.

"He is aching at the courthouse," she informed, being somewhat mixed up concerning the information I had given her.

Actually, she was correct in one respect, because I was aching considerably at the Aiken Courthouse that week.

## *Judicial Floating*

Not long after I was first elected Judge of the Seventh Judicial Circuit, Spartanburg American Legion Post 28—of which I was a member—decided to participate in the Christmas parade.

We had to supply Legionnaires to walk about mid-distance between the numerous commercial floats. Every veteran thus participating was requested to wear his Legion cap.

The time was soon after the end of World War II, when veterans were being particularly recognized and invited to participate in many functions. I agreed to help out and made the long walk between two commercial floats.

Soon thereafter, a friend said he was glad to see me taking part.

"There's a new day in the administration of justice in Spartanburg," he rejoiced. "This is the first time—and it wasn't until after Littlejohn was elected— that the Seventh Judicial Circuit entered a float in the Christmas parade."

Judges are called many names, but that was the only time I've ever been called anything as mild as a Christmas float.

## *A Judge By Any Other Name*

When I became a circuit judge in 1949, no judicial office space was available for me at Spartanburg County Courthouse. Accordingly, I moved into the nearby Montgomery Building and headquartered there until the new courthouse was completed in 1958.

I had a sign painter inscribe on the door of this temporary office, "Seventh Judicial Circuit, Judge's Chambers."

One day some people from near Lyman came to see me and walked down the hall outside, looking for the office of Judge Littlejohn. They failed to find a door bearing my name, so I heard one of them suggest, "Let's go in here. Maybe Judge Chambers can tell us how to find him."

* * *

My good friend, Dr. P. B. Connor, a dentist, operated his office across the hall from mine. On his door was printed, "P. B. Connor, D.D.S., Periodontist." He was, of course, a specialist in treatment of diseases of the gums. One day a man came to my office, and as he left he read the sign and commented, "It must be mighty nice to have a foot doctor this close by, just in case you need him."

Thereafter, Doctor Connor called me Judge Chambers and I called him podiatrist—or Foot Doctor Connor.

## *"The Horse's Mouth"*

It is not unusual for a citizen to approach a judge, seeking advice. He reasons that he should receive good counsel—and free.

Not long after I had been elected circuit judge, a friend from Boiling Springs in my home county of Spartanburg telephoned and wanted me to advise him relative to a landlord and tenant problem confronting him.

I told him what I have told hundreds of people over the years, to this effect: "I am not permitted to practice law. I can't advise you about this question any more than I could advise the people on the other side." I then suggested that if he had a legal problem, the proper thing for him to do was to choose an attorney and seek his advice.

He responded, "Well, Judge, I have already talked to several lawyers and I didn't like what any of them told me, so I wanted to come to you and get it straight from the horse's mouth."

## *Leniency In Reverse*

I was born and reared in the little town of Pacolet, ten miles from Spartanburg.

When I was attending the local grammar school, there was a young fellow in my class whom we called "Willy." He dropped out of school when he reached the eighth or ninth grade. About a year later he was in trouble with the law. A suspended sentence gave him another chance, but within a few months he was charged with another violation. This cost him a short sentence. He was released and repeated his lawbreaking. Willy was in and out of jail for fifteen or eighteen years.

He was weak where temptation was concerned. He'd write a check to get money when he had no funds in the bank. Occasionally, he'd steal a typewriter or some other article. Once or twice he married some gal who was supposed to have money, but mostly he kept in trouble.

In 1950, when I was about to hold my first court in Spartanburg, I learned my friend Willy was in the county jail. He had been in trouble so often and had skipped bail so often that nobody would sign his bond.

On Saturday before court was to be convened on Monday, I received a letter, written with pencil on plain white paper and enclosed in a plain white envelope, this being the kind of stationery furnished to prisoners awaiting trial. The communication was from Willy. He wrote, informally and pathetically:

"Dear Bruce, I am now waiting trial in the county jail and my case is going to come up before you. Over the years I have read about you becoming a lawyer. I read that you went to the legislature. It looks like everything you have attempted has been successful. Now, me, it looks like I just have trouble all the time. I've been on probation. I've skipped bond. I've served time and now I'm down here charged with forging nine checks.

"Fate has been unkind to me," he lamented. "Fate has been kind to you. But for fate, the shoe might be on the other foot. It could have been you that would be in jail and I would be the judge; and if it had so happened, I just wanted you to know that I would put you on probation."

## *Mischief Backfired*

When I became a circuit judge in 1949, I left the law firm of Odom, Bostick, Littlejohn and Nolen.

At that time I had been in politics about thirteen years and had just taken the oath of office as judge. I was well-known over the county, and especially at the old post office close by. Having left the law firm, it was necessary for me to rent my own postal mailbox so I went to the post office and applied for one. A postal employee gave me a form to fill out and said they could not rent me a box without first checking my references. He suggested that I write the names of two people who knew me on the card. This seemed a bit foolish to me, because I knew nearly everybody in the post office personally and they knew me. But I put down two names, those of my cousin Broadus Littlejohn of the Community Cash Stores and Frank Bostick, my former law partner.

A few days later Frank received a form inquiry through the mail about me. He knew that I was personally acquainted with nearly everybody at the post office and also thought it was rather foolish, and instead of answering the questions he mischievously wrote a message in long hand across the form.

My law partner mailed this back to the post office where it ended up on the desk of Wade Hughston, the postmaster. Next day the postmaster came personally to Frank's office, disturbed about the matter, and asked him to fill out a replacement form.

"Why Wade, you know Bruce as well as I do," Frank replied. "Why do you need a recommendation to rent him a post office box?"

Mr. Hughston explained, “Frank, these cards end up in Washington, and if you don’t withdraw this one. I will have to send it to Washington. And when I report to them that I have rented a box to a man whose references didn’t pan out, I will have to write a hundred letters explaining why. You can simplify it for me if you will withdraw this card and fill out another one correctly.”

Frank complied.

After the postmaster had left, the secretary asked Frank what he had written on the card. Frank replied, “All I said was, ‘I have never heard of this character in my life. Why should he want a mailbox?’ ”

# "THE DEFENDANT SAYETH"

## *Fickleness Under Fire*

While I was holding court in Bamberg in the spring of 1950, a young man charged with assault and battery with intent to kill came before me to enter a guilty plea.

The facts presented showed that the prosecuting witness and the defendant were courting the same girl. An interesting feature of the evidence was that the rural area house where the girl lived still had a kitchen door with a cat hole in it, and this opening had figured in the assault. For the information of moderns, a cat hole in the earlier days was an opening cut at the bottom of a kitchen door to permit the family cat to enter or leave at will, without human assistance.

Anyway, the accused was unhappy because another young man was visiting his girlfriend, so he went to the house, poked the barrel of his shotgun through the cat hole, and when his competitor (who was inside) walked close to the door with the girl, the accused fired the load of shot into his competitor's leg, inflicting a serious wound.

The case worried me, because young people and a competitive courtship were involved; yet I realized the shotgunning swain had to receive a substantial sentence. I was still pondering the extent of punishment when the victim completed his testimony and started walking back to his seat in the courtroom.

Suddenly he stopped, returned to the front of the room, stood before the clerk's desk and informed me, "Judge, there's one other thing I'd like to tell you about this case."

This pleased me, because I thought he was going to volunteer information that would ease my sentencing problem. "That's fine," I invited him, "Just go ahead and tell me anything else you want me to know."

He paused and then informed the court, "Judge, after this thing happened, that gal done quit us both and got herself a new boy friend."

## *Swapping "Legalized"*

During a 1953 criminal court term in Charleston, a defendant named Jones pleaded guilty before me to charges of issuing several fraudulent checks.

Before passing sentence, I asked him several questions in an effort to determine the appropriate sentence; I also inquired if there was anything he wanted to tell me about the case.

"Yes, sir, Judge," he quickly responded, "if you can put me on probation, I think I'm gonna get along all right now. I done got rid of that woman."

No woman had been mentioned during the proceeding, as I hastened to point out. "I haven't heard about any woman in this case. Who are you talking about?"

"It's my wife," he answered. "She just married me for spite anyhow, but I done got rid of her and things are going to be all right now."

Curiously I inquired, "Who was she attempting to spite—herself or you?"

"It weren't either one," he explained. "My first wife married her first husband, and it made her so mad she married me."

At least they had made their swapping legal.

## *He Finally Won One*

Around 1964 a young man named Phillip pleaded guilty before me to a charge of assault and battery upon his wife.

I asked the wife to tell me exactly what had happened. She related that Phillip had been drinking whiskey while "out on the town" and had returned home about two a. m. She said she had an injured leg and was walking with the aid of a crutch, which was under her bed. They quarreled and engaged in some name-calling, then Phillip grabbed the crutch and struck her across the back with it.

Giving her husband his turn, I inquired, "Phillip, what do you have to say for yourself?"

"Judge, she tell it about right," he readily admitted but he added, "I want to tell you what our real trouble is. We live over there in a nest full of kinfolks. Every which way I turn there is one of them in-laws trying to tell me what to do. If there was such a thing as us moving out and away from this nest full of kinfolks and in-laws, I believe we could get along all right. The truth of the matter is, we've been living over there for five years, we've been married for five years, and we've been fighting for five years."

He paused and implored, "Judge, we've been fighting for five years and I ain't never won yet, unless you let me come out on top today."

I was impressed with his plight and placed him on probation.

## *Communication Expanded*

Sometimes a witness may feel that he is not getting through to the jury.

I was hearing criminal cases and Solicitor Rufus Fant was prosecuting over in Anderson, when a man on the stand apparently sought to remedy this deficiency.

Mr. Fant was very courteous as well as efficient. He frequently addressed a witness as "Mr. Witness."

In this instance, Mr. Fant asked a question which the witness ducked. Instead he interjected two or three other questions on his own and provided answers to them which were very damaging to the prosecutor's case.

Solicitor Fant sought to get him back on the track. "Mr. Witness," he pointed out, "I didn't ask you that."

"I know you didn't," the witness replied, "but I wanted the jury to know about it."

## *He Loved And Lost*

Once, during Sam Watt's long career as solicitor of the Seventh Judicial Circuit, he was prosecuting a girl named Emma on a grand larceny charge.

The prosecuting witness was a salesman who said he had checked in at a Spartanburg hotel and met Emma in a local restaurant. They communicated so ardently that they ended up in his hotel room. The salesman complained that when he awoke the following morning Emma was gone, along with $150 from his wallet.

Usually, most salesmen thus penalized for pleasure would chalk it off to experience, lick their wounds sorrowfully and keep quiet—but not this fellow. He had learned who Emma was and proceeded to sign a warrant charging her with grand larceny.

In court she pleaded not guilty, whereupon Solicitor Watt, cross-examining her, inquired, "Now Emma, this salesman says you all drank a Coca Cola and that he can't swear to it but he believes you put knockout drops in his Coke and caused him to pass out; then while he was passed out, you took his money. Now, I ask you, Emma, did you put knockout drops in his Coca Cola?"

"No, Mr. Solicitor," the damsel fired back, "When I get through with them, they don't need no knockout drops!"

## *Thirsty Kinfolk*

When there is no good answer to a question, a defendant must often content himself with submitting a highly unsatisfactory one. Sometimes persons caught with illegal liquor in their possession come up with some unusual explanations and excuses.

I had before me a man who was pleading guilty to violating the liquor law. "How long have you been selling liquor?" I asked him.

Selling liquor is a more serious offense and carries a stiffer sentence than simple possession. Obviously the accused knew this, and he hastened to straighten me out on the facts by saying, "Judge, I've never sold any liquor. This was for my own use."

I turned to the sheriff and inquired, "How much did he have?"

The sheriff smiled at the defendant, then looked at me and responded, "Seventeen gallons."

An explanation was obviously needed, and the defendant knew this immediately. He promptly explained: "Judge, I am kin to nearly everybody what live in my territory. I was saving it up for a party. When my kinfolks come to see me they don't bring nothing, and when we have a party they expect me to furnish the liquor. I was trying to save up enough so we could celebrate together."

## *Frightened Feet*

During the first few years of my circuit judgeship, we tried a lot of cases in which defendants were charged with manufacturing illegal whisky.

One defendant brought before me when I was presiding in McCormick had been seen by the sheriff at a still. Actually, he had been almost caught beside the boilers, but when the sheriff spotted the culprit he had run.

This didn't cause the sheriff any problem. He recognized the distiller and so didn't chase him. He just leisurely arrested him at his convenience.

After the defendant had pleaded guilty, I ask him, "Why did you run? You must have known that the sheriff recognized you and would get you later."

"Judge, it wasn't my fault," he explained. "I wanted to stay, but my feet just wouldn't stand still."

## *Interdenominational*

During a term of criminal court in Darlington, a man about fifty years old was being tried before me on a charge of stealing a bale of cotton.

He worked at a warehouse where cotton was stored and occasionally, with the help of one or two fellow workmen, he would take a bale of cotton out of the warehouse, run it through the sales office and have the boss give them a check for it. The bale would then be returned to the warehouse.

Near the end of the day when the jurors reported their verdict, no spectators remained in the courtroom. Only the clerk and lawyers involved in the case were there. I questioned the defendant briefly concerning his background, noting among other things, "I have observed in the trial of this case that they have called you 'preacher.' Are you a preacher or is that just a nickname?"

"Yes sir, Judge," he confirmed, "I'm a preacher."

"What kind of preacher are you?" I asked.

"I'm a Methodist preacher," he informed me.

Indulging lightly in levity—which a judge does not do if he has an audience—I observed, "Well, preacher, I'm sorry to hear that you're a Methodist. I'm a Baptist, and though I would not intentionally sentence a Methodist to a longer term than I would a Baptist, it's just conceivable that without meaning to be unfair about it, I might impose a greater sentence."

Quickly the nimble-minded defendant exclaimed, "Mr. Judge, Your Honor, just to tell the truth about it, I does some Baptist preaching, too."

## *Jurisdiction Jumble*

I was presiding over Union County General Sessions Court at a late 1950s May term when a defendant named Carter, charged with assault and battery of a high and aggravated nature upon his wife, stood before me.

According to the evidence, he had chained her to a rocking chair to make sure that she stayed at home. Some of my friends there facetiously remarked that he was entitled to some consideration, because he could have chained her to a straight chair. Anyway, I imposed a probationary sentence.

This developed into one of those cases that make judges old before their time. The defendant wasn't well-balanced mentally, and he wasn't mean enough to rate penitentiary confinement.

He proceeded thereafter to pester various judges with complaints about his probation. He wanted its terms changed.

He contacted another circuit judge in Union. After this judge had left the circuit and returned to his home, Carter pursued him further by telephone. He was told by his judicial target, "I can no longer consider your case, because I am out of your jurisdiction. You'll have to see Judge Littlejohn."

Carter immediately headed in my direction, further burdened with a misunderstanding of what the other judge had told him. To me he said:

"That other judge said he would help me but he was out with Doris Dixon."

### *Expediter*

Third Judicial Circuit Solicitor Kirk McLeod stands out in my experience as one of the strongest and most diligent public prosecutors in South Carolina, both as an expediter of proceedings and a procurer of guilty pleas.

We were opening a General Sessions term one Monday morning at Kingstree. This was shortly before the case of *Gideon vs. Wainwright* was decided by the U. S. Supreme Court, making it necessary for just about every defendant to have a lawyer. Grand jurors were just beginning their task and Mr. McLeod, holding a thick pack of indictments, proceeded to call the names of defendants present and to inquire into their preferences or wishes concerning the disposition of their cases. He called the first case: "Willy Wilson, if you are present, will you stand up."

Willy stood. The solicitor addressed him: "You are charged with the larceny of an automobile. Do you plead guilty or not guilty?"

This defendant wanted to plead guilty and was instructed, "Sit down. I'll take your plea a little later."

Continuing, the solicitor called out, "Casper West, will you stand up. You're charged with assault and battery with intent to kill. Are you going to plead guilty or not guilty?"

West responded, "I'm going to plead not guilty," whereupon the solicitor directed, "Sit down. I'll give you a trial later in the day."

Next defendant Charlie Westbrook was requested to stand. The solicitor addressed him, "In this indictment you are charged with the offense of rape. Do you want to plead guilty or not guilty?"

Charlie didn't take either route.

Instead, he said, "Mr. Solicitor, I want to settle out of court, please."

## *Tribute "Tenderizes"*

Nowadays not many persons are charged with manufacturing, selling or possessing illegal liquor, but many years ago such cases were plentiful on the state's criminal dockets.

Many court terms ago a man pleaded guilty before me to a charge of possessing several gallons. I discerned from the evidence that he was a moonshine merchandiser, because nobody had that much around for personal use. Accordingly, before sentencing him I inquired, "How long have you been dealing in white liquor?"

He promptly proclaimed piously, "This is the first time, Judge."

Delving further, I asked him, "How does it happen that all of the defendants charged with violating the liquor law always tell me that they got caught the first time?"

Veteran Sheriff B. B. Brockman of Spartanburg was still in office at the time and seated in a chair in the empty jury box. The defendant looked at him, smiled, then turned back to me and said, "Judge, I guess it's because we've got such a fine sheriff he can catch 'em the first time."

"Sheriff," I asked Mr. Brockman, "what you got to say about that?"

The sheriff smiled and admitted, "Judge, he may not be as bad as I thought he was."

## *He Keeps Me In Stitches*

In Greenville a defendant pleaded guilty before me to a charge of assault and battery with intent to kill with a knife.

Before sentencing, I queried the victim, who supposedly was the prosecuting witness, and found him non-committal.

"Judge, it might have been an accident," he said.

Realizing that the court had an unwilling witness, I insisted, "Well, even so, just go ahead and tell me what happened."

He responded weakly, "Judge, it might have been mostly my fault."

Aware that we were trying to pump from a dry well, I shifted to Solicitor Jim Mann and asked, "Solicitor, how many stitches?"

He was much more informative. "Judge, there were one hundred fourteen," he said. Then he added, "We see this in court all the time. The truth of the matter is, this witness wanted to drop the charge and the State wouldn't let him. They got together and have tried to make up. The defendant has promised the prosecuting witness that if he will help make it light on him, he will pay the doctor's bill. That's why he doesn't want to tell you anything about it."

I pursued "Mr. Solicitor, do you think it was an accident?"

"No, sir, Your Honor, I know how you feel about these cutting cases, and if you didn't put this man on the chain gang, I would think *that* was an accident."

## *Supporting Evidence*

A Laurens County Criminal Court jury convicted a young man of deserting and failing to support his wife and small children. Such a case usually called for a suspended sentence, conditioned upon the husband's providing weekly support money for his dependents. When the time came to impose the sentence, the defendant's wife was present and eager to supply additional information.

During pre-sentence questioning I told him, "In the evidence before the court and the jury, I heard talk of another woman. Tell me about her. Who is she?"

He hedged. "That's my wife's talk," he insisted. "She's just mad at me."

His mate began mowing him down, like shooting birds on the ground, by declaring, "Judge, her name is Nellie Westbrook."

Hubby hedged some more, "When a woman gets mad at you, she'll say anything."

"She's downstairs waiting for him now," the wife fired back.

"Judge, I wouldn't do a thing like that," he contended.

"Judge, she's sitting in a blue Ford," the wife informed me.

"I don't even have a blue Ford," he said, still dodging her accusations.

"Of course he doesn't have a blue Ford, Judge. It belongs to his daddy."

Hubby hedged still another time, "She's just mad at me. She'll say anything to get more money."

The wife red flagged this strategy. "Judge, the blue Ford with Nellie Westbrook in it is sitting in front of the Rexall Store across the street, and she's waiting for him."

I decided to place the defendant on the spot and told him, "I am going to make you a sporting proposition. I have been attempting to determine whether you ought to pay twenty-five dollars per week or thirty dollars per week. Now, I'm going to send Bailiff Joe Medlock out to see if Nellie Westbrook is sitting in a blue Ford in front of the Rexall Store across the street, and if she is you can pay thirty dollars a week. If she's not sitting in the blue Ford in front of the Rexall Store across the street, I'll let you pay twenty-five dollars."

Medlock departed the courtroom, and you could hear a pin drop as all persons present awaited his return. He hurried back, smiling, and gave his report.

The husband looked sheepish. He paid thirty dollars a week.

## *Changing Gears*

Handling domestic relations cases is among the most unpleasant tasks confronting judges. They're apt to present almost every kind of problem, some of them very personal.

One of these proceedings coming before me as circuit judge involved a couple in their late forties. They had been married about twenty-five years, and their troubles seemed to be of recent origin.

The husband pleaded guilty to deserting his wife and failing to support their children. As usual, I sought to persuade them to reconcile their differences and reestablish their home by asking, "What seems to be the trouble?" and making other inquiries.

The wife wouldn't respond, but finally the husband stammered, "Judge, she's changing gears."

I was tempted to ask him, "What gear was she in and what gear is she shifting to?" but decided not to be facetious for fear of adding to her mechanical difficulties.

## *Too Much To Handle*

A man about twenty-two was charged in criminal court at Greenville with desertion and non-support of his wife and one small child. Actually, it was evident from the wife's appearance that they had one-and-a-half children.

She was about twenty, blonde, beautiful and buxom. I looked her over carefully, as is the duty of a judge under such circumstances.

After the testimony was completed, I felt an impulse to try to keep them together. "Have you attempted to reconcile your differences?" I inquired. I then counseled, "The law appreciates the fact that it is better for couples to be united rather than be separated. It looks to me like you are the type of couple that just ought to be able to get along." Then I asked again, "Have you attempted to reconcile your differences?"

Neither answered, so I inquired further. "What seems to be the real trouble that you aren't able to get along?"

Again they stood silent.

Still trying, I looked the husband straight in the eye and asked him, "Young man, you got another woman?"

He looked at me sort of innocent-like and uttered a question of his own, "Judge, what do I need with another woman?" Then he looked at her and back at me and said, "I got more woman right here than what I can handle."

I looked at her again, concluded he was telling the truth, and disposed of the case without any further effort to reconcile them.

## *Bossman*

I was holding a term of court in Williamsburg County and had sent a jury out to deliberate its verdict late in the afternoon.

The probation officer approached the bench. "Your Honor," he said, "I have in court a young man charged with violating his probation. He has been sitting here all day at my direction, awaiting the possibility of a hearing."

I invited the officer to bring the probationer forward for the purpose of determining whether his probation should be revoked. He called a young man about twenty-five years of age from the spectators area. When he came forward I recognized him as one who had appeared restless in court all day, squirming around at his seat.

"Your Honor," the probation officer informed me, "when Judge J. B. Pruitt of Anderson was here about two years ago, he sentenced this young man for stealing a mule. The sentence was that he should serve three months in confinement and thereafter be on probation for three years. After he had served the three months sentence, instead of reporting to the probation officer as he was directed to do, he left the state and went to Florida, where he stayed about a year. He returned recently and has abused his wife. I submit that he has violated his probation by leaving the state without permission and by mistreating his wife."

I was intrigued by the fact that anyone would steal a mule, and so I turned to the probationer and said, "Young man, why did you steal a mule? Of all the things in the world a man ought not to steal in these modern times, it's a mule. There are so few of them left that everyone takes notice of who has one. You can't sell them; you can't rent them; you can't work them enough to make money out of them; you can't hide them and you've got to feed them. Mules are so conspicuous that you might just as well steal a red, white and blue elephant. I can't understand why anybody would steal a mule. Can you explain?"

"Bossman," the probationer pleaded, "I know I did wrong, but I will never do it again, Bossman. If you will make it easy on me this time, Bossman, you never will have any trouble with me again. Bossman, if you let me go this time, the law will never be troubled by me again as long as I live. I guarantee you that, Bossman."

I inquired, "Let me ask you something. Why do you call me Bossman?"

"Because, if I ever in my life had a bossman, you is it."

* * *

About that time the jury returned its verdict and interrupted my probation hearing. When the jury had gone, I quietly called the probation officer to the bench and told him that I was not sure that this fellow had all of his marbles and inquired what he thought I ought to do with him.

The probation officer replied, "I am not seriously asking that his probation be revoked, but I sure couldn't overlook his actions without at least having him report to you."

We were in agreement and I directed, "Just go back there and tell this young man that the judge said to go and sin no more, and that all is forgiven."

The message obviously delighted the worried mule thief. He smiled, walked to the rear door, then turned and walked back down the aisle in front of the clerk's desk, looked up at me, smiled again even broader, and waved with a sort of "I thank you" gesture. The courtroom was almost empty, and my mother had always told me not to let anyone be nicer to me than I was to him, so I couldn't resist the temptation of waving back at him. When I did, he turned and walked out of the courtroom without looking back. I terminated his case. The court lost a probationer, and a probationer lost a bossman.

## *Common Law Divorce*

During a Greenville term of criminal court, I was questioning a defendant preparatory to passing sentence.

Recalling that something had been said about his having two wives, I asked him, "How long has your first wife been dead? Or are you divorced?"

He answered, "Yes, sir, we've got a common law divorce."

I was well familiar with common law marriages, but I had never heard of a common law divorce, so I warmed up to him with, "Tell me about that common law divorce. How does it work?"

He detailed it as follows: "Well, Judge, me and my first old lady got married down at the probate judge's office and we got a certificate. That's what you call a paper wedding. After we had been married about four years, she take off and shack up with another man. And so I asked some of 'em about it and they tell me, 'That cuts you loose.' So I married again."

## *Husbands And Liquor*

Husbands drinking too much liquor are the source of a lot of law business on the criminal side of the court. There seems to be a tendency to violate the law when one gets a few too many under the belt, and I have often been amused at what the defendants and witnesses say about the habit when indulged to excess.

In Anderson a man pleaded guilty before me on a charge of driving under the influence. When I asked him why he had downed so much whiskey, he had this unique explanation:

"Judge, I work down at the coal yard. The coal dust settles on my lungs and I have to drink a little liquor to keep the dust washed out of them."

* * *

On another occasion, I dealt with a husband whose liquid problem caused financial difficulty. He was charged with nonsupport of his wife and children.

The wife testified that the problems were chiefly caused by gulping gulley liquor. He drank heavily, she said.

I inquired, "Lady, when does he do all this drinking?"

She replied, "Mostly during the weekend and during the week."

* * *

Arthur Estes, a very capable probation officer at Spartanburg in the 1950s, brought a twenty-eight-year-old man before me, asking that I revoke his probation because he had been leaving home and getting drunk regularly every weekend. His wife testified that every Friday he would begin imbibing and continue through Sunday. He didn't have money enough to buy the liquor he consumed and feed his family too, and so the family suffered. This was a violation of his probation.

After his wife had explained this to me, I asked, "Fellow, what do you have to say about this?"

"Judge, she tell it about right," he readily admitted, but added, "the real trouble between me and the old lady is that she is a genuine double-dipped prohibitionist. I can't stay home and drink like a gentleman, because she raises so much cain. After I work hard all week, I feel like I have got to have a little drink to keep my blood circulating. I go off on Friday and first thing you know I take a drink and it makes me feel like a new man. Then the new man wants a drink, and first thing you know I am drunk." Then he implored, "Judge, I want you to do something for me."

"What's that?" I asked.

"I want you to put my wife on probation," he pleaded, "you tell her what she got to do is let me take a little drink at home. If I could just stay home and drink with respectability, I wouldn't go off and get drunk like a fool."

I refused his request, explaining to him that he was my problem but that his wife was his problem.

# DOMESTIC TRANQUILITY

## *Ethical Romancing*

During World War II there was a shortage of doctors in the Army but always a surplus of lawyers. In fact, the Army had so many lawyers they all could not go into the Judge Advocate General Department, where most of us attorneys would have preferred to be. And so lawyers were sent to the Artillery, the Quartermaster Corps and all the other departments.

It fell my lot to be assigned at first to the Quartermaster Corps, which basically feeds and clothes the Army. I was assigned to Camp Lee, Virginia, for training. Men were trained there in warehousing and laundry supply and to be truck drivers and mess sergeants and for various other duties.

When fellows in the Army learned I had been a lawyer in civilian life, it was not unusual for them to ask legal advice on all sorts of matters.

One day in the barracks at Camp Lee, Virginia, a New Yorker who had been assigned to truck drivers school came to my bunk and inquired, “Say, Littlejohn, weren’t you a lawyer back home?”

I told him, “Yes, Mr. Kosch, I practiced law for seven years before coming into the Army.”

He proceeded to detail his pathetic personal case by wishing “there was something you could do to help me. My family up in New York is about to starve to death. The Red Cross gives them about fifteen or twenty dollars a month, and that ain’t enough to live on. I’m greatly concerned.”

Now Kosch could not read or write, and when he entered the Army, he didn’t have a tooth in his head. His captain had sent him to the dental clinic, where he was outfitted with a brand new set of plates. I think they were his first.

Kosch was about thirty-eight, just barely under the maximum age for Army acceptance. When he got his new teeth, I have never seen a fellow more proud. He returned to the barracks, grinning and showing his uppers and lowers as though he were going to bite everybody there just to prove he had them.

Anyway, I told him, "Kosch, of course your folks can't live on Red Cross money" and advised, "Why don't you give them an allotment?" Under regulations, a soldier could allot twenty-eight dollars a month; the Army would add twenty-two dollars and send fifty dollars a month to the wife or other designated dependent.

Kosch's problem didn't fit this solution. "Me and the old lady never was exactly married," he admitted. "Up in New York they don't recognize a common law marriage. If they did, the Army would recognize it and I could get the allotment." I asked him what his family consisted of. "Well," he counted off, "there's the old lady. And then I got a daughter what's fifteen years old, and I got another daughter what's seventeen years old."

This predicament called for special counseling. "This is what I think you ought to do," I suggested. "Ask the captain to give you a three-day pass. It's only three hundred miles to New York. Go home and propose to this lady you've been living with all this time and get married to her. Bring your marriage certificate back, turn it in to the orderly room, and next month she'll be getting an allotment."

Kosch disappeared the next day, and I learned he had received his pass and gone to New York. Three days later he returned, apparently better satisfied, so I went to his bunk and inquired, "How are you getting along? Did you get married like I told you to?"

He hadn't, but he had this explanation: "No, I tell you how it is. I went home and found out something I never had knowed before. About twenty years ago my old lady married another man. He disappeared. When I asked her to marry me, she said she didn't know where this husband was or whether he was dead or alive. She said she was afraid that if she married me he might turn up and then the law would get her for bigamy. And my old lady, she don't want to do nothing what's wrong."

## *Bridal Bridge Burning*

In 1942 Camp Croft, an infantry installation where soldiers were trained for combat, was in full operation. At that time I had not yet entered the Army and was still practicing law in nearby Spartanburg.

One night a local girl telephoned me, seeking advice. I asked what her problem was and she responded:

"I married one of those soldiers out at Camp Croft. They shipped him out and I think he's gone to Italy. I don't know when he's coming back. He may never come back."

I asked her to detail her problem more specifically.

"Well," she said, "after we got married down at the probate judge's office, I got all the papers. He hasn't got a scratch of the pen. Now, what I want to know, Mr. Littlejohn, is if I burn all those papers up, won't I be single again?"

## *Tethered By Love*

The Spartanburg County Jail cells are located on the second floor, enabling prisoners to view the jail-courthouse parking lot.

It is not unusual for prisoners who have little else to do to yell at people who are parking their cars preparatory to entering the courthouse. It is also not unusual for young couples wanting to get married to show up at the courthouse at nine a. m. sharp and head for the office of Probate Judge J. William Davenport to apply for their license. I usually arrive about the same time and have seen many young couples leave their cars and walk in the direction of the probate office.

One morning a youthful couple parked near where I had just left my car. They joined hands, smiled, began swinging their hands back and forth happily and started walking toward the courthouse, two more "customers" for Judge Davenport.

At this point, a "smart guy" yelled from his cell, "Hey, Buddy, turn her hand loose. She won't go anywhere."

The startled swain dropped the hand of his bride-to-be as though he had received a command.

But the jail bird was right.

She did not go anywhere!

## *Downstairs To Delight*

Never a day passes without a number of young couples coming to Spartanburg County Courthouse in search of the Probate Judge for the purpose of getting married.

Most of them are understandably excited; usually they are embarking upon the matrimonial sea for the first time.

Once I was standing in the lobby when a young couple entered. Holding hands, they approached the information desk and asked a question. The girl at the desk obviously told them that the Probate Judge's office was in a certain numbered room downstairs. They walked away and came back near where I was standing. Two stairways were nearby. One went up to the next floor and the other went down to the floor where the judge's office is located.

A bit mixed-up, they tried out a stairway, then paused. They looked at the ceiling, then at the directory board and finally at me.

Sensing their plight, I inquired, "Can I help you find someone?"

Obviously, the young lady meant to ask me, "Which way is it to the Probate Judge's office?" Instead, in her frustration, she just said, "Mister, which way is downstairs?"

## *Bedfellow Not Qualified*

A woman had her boy friend prosecuted for failure to support three children born to her. They were not married.

Miss Folsom Smith, Seventh Judicial Circuit court reporter, relates this incident before another judge who was presiding in Spartanburg.

It developed, as the judge was endeavoring to determine how much maintenance money should be paid by the father, that he and the woman were still living together.

This prompted the judge to inquire, "Wouldn't this matter be settled better if you two just went ahead and got married? How long have you been living together?"

The woman said "five or six years," and the judge asked her individually, "Wouldn't it be better if you just got married?"

But the woman was not cooperative. "No, I can't marry him," she said.

"Why can't you marry him?" the judge wanted to know.

She replied, "Because he drinks liquor."

## *Electrocution Preferred*

Under South Carolina's divorce law, cases are tried without a jury. More frequently, testimony is given before the master in equity or a special referee and recorded in question-and-answer form. This hearing official then transmits the testimony with his recommendation to a judge for his review. In Union County, Probate Judge Kennedy was also master in equity. He heard numerous divorce cases and transmitted the records to me when his county was part of my Seventh Judicial Circuit.

One record he transmitted to me had a unique ending.

The law requires that the hearing official must attempt to reconcile the husband and wife, and certification that this was done is necessary before a divorce can be granted. In this case the wife was the plaintiff. Most husbands are in default in these cases, but this time the defendant was in court—not to contest the awarding of a decree but apparently to make sure that she received it.

When the testimony was completed, Judge Kennedy counseled the couple: "Under the law, I am required to attempt to reconcile you. Isn't there something I could say or do that would help to bring about a reconciliation? The law recognizes the fact that it is better for a couple to live together than to be divorced, and it would give me much pleasure if I could just do something along this line that would be helpful to both of you. Isn't there something I could say or do that would put you all back together again, under the same roof?"

The husband dismissed the judicial pleadings with this response: "Judge, I had rather you put me in the electric chair."

Judge Kennedy's record reflected no further inquiries, answers or comments, and he crisply concluded:

"The hearing is ended."

## *"Excuse Me!"*

Romance in the raw is seldom mild. Love can and oftentimes does fire up wrath, and sometimes the results are tragic. In a criminal case at Conway, a young man was charged with assault and battery with intent to kill. As the evidence unfolded, it revealed that the defendant and a red-headed young man were competing for the affections of a pretty blonde. The redhead and the blonde had been attending a dance at the Myrtle Beach Pavilion. The defendant, angry with her as well as with his rival, had gone to the pavilion in hopes of advancing his own interests.

The defendant waited outside the pavilion until the music stopped. About that time a red-headed fellow came through the door. The defendant, fuming from anger and jealousy, jumped from behind a bush and raked a switchblade knife across the redhead's throat inflicting a serious but non-fatal wound.

Stunned and disabled, the red-headed fellow dropped his head, obscuring his face. The defendant grabbed him by the hair and raised his head for a clearer view of his face.

Then he exclaimed, "Excuse me, you ain't the one."

## *Cooperative Acquiesence*

Once I stopped at a service station in Columbia to buy gasoline. The attendant, about twenty-five, saw my "F-2" license plate number and asked, "Say, mister, aren't you a judge?"

"I believe I am," I admitted, and continued, "And I bet I know why you knew it. You were up in my court one time, weren't you?"

He smiled and said, "No sir, Judge, I ain't never been in court and I ain't never gonna be there as long as I live."

"You feel rather confident about it," I noted. "How can you be so sure?"

He allowed, "I may have troubles one of these days, but being in court is not one of 'em."

His certainty was fascinating, so I explored a bit, "How do you know you aren't going to have woman trouble?"

"Oh, Judge," he assured me, "now that's one trouble I know I ain't gonna have as long as I live."

"How can you be so sure?" I inquired.

He readily replied, "I'm gonna give in."

## *Romance On The Rocks*

Striving to solve domestic relations disputes can give a judge gray hair or cost him some of the hair he still has. But sometimes the disputes produce humor which sparks the long days in court and makes the task endurable.

Once, while wrestling with a divorce proceeding, I asked the complaining wife, "Actually, what you are seeking is alimony, isn't it?"

She promptly exclaimed, "No, sir. What do I want with alimony? I'm getting all he makes now."

Spotting her as the boss of the household, I pointedly inquired, "Lady, do you think that you henpeck your husband?"

She responded belligerently, "No, sir. As long as he does what I tell him to do, I'll never henpeck him."

## *A Pint Of Nothing*

On one occasion, a man pleaded guilty before me on a charge of failing to support his wife.

I was considering the routine disposition in such cases—a sentence suspended during probation with the provision that he support her—but first I asked, "What seems to be the trouble? Why haven't you been doing more for your wife?"

Defensively he replied, "Judge, I buyed her a hotpint stove."

She discarded his "generosity" by declaring, "Yes, Judge, but he didn't buy me a pint of nothing to hot on it."

## *Booze, Bite First*

A husband-father defendant pleaded guilty before me to desertion and non-support. It is customary to impose a probationary sentence in such cases, leaving the husband free to work and requiring him to pay stipulated sums each week for the support of his dependents. This requires the presiding judge to inquire into the defendant's earning capacity and the needs of his wife and children.

In this case, as usual, I asked the wife, "How much money does he make?"

"I don't know," she admitted. "He doesn't ever tell me."

I persisted. "Well, you must know approximately how much he makes. About how much do you think it is? Have you ever heard him mention it?"

"No," she replied, "he don't ever tell me none of his business."

The solicitor, trying to assist, asked her, "Mary, what's his take-home pay?"

She said, "Well, that depend on whether he get drunk 'fore he get home."

## *Love Taps*

Back in the 1950s I was holding General Sessions Court in Camden and it was pleas day.

A young corporal from Fort Jackson pleaded guilty to a second offense charge of driving under the influence.

He came to court obviously hoping to impress the judge. Every hair on his head was precisely in place, his trousers were neatly pressed and his tie was tucked into his shirt just right; he was truly an immaculate soldier. Standing beside him was a pretty woman, also immaculately attired.

The state highway patrolman who had made the arrest stated the facts and then volunteered, "Judge, I did not make a case against this young man for assault and battery, but I think I should call your attention to the fact that when I arrested him his wife was with him and she had been beaten. Her clothes were torn, her hair was disheveled and she had undergone a rough ordeal. But I figured that if I charged him with assault and battery, she wouldn't testify against him and I couldn't prove the case, so I just let it stop at a driving under the influence charge."

"Corporal, is it true that you have beaten your wife in the manner described to the court," I asked him. He didn't reply but his wife interposed, "Judge, it might have been mostly my fault."

Realizing the court had two unwilling witnesses, I inquired further, "Well, even so, did he beat you some?"

Hesitantly, she murmured, "Really, it wasn't . . . I don't know that I can say he did."

"Would you say that he struck you once or twice, more or less gently?" I asked.

Shyly, she said, "Judge, we ain't been married long. Whatever he did to me was just that first year's adjustment taking place."

## *Evidence Buried*

One of the first murder cases I tried was in Aiken. Bert Carter was solicitor. The indictment charged a woman with slaying her husband. She did not have an attorney so I appointed Bennie Surasky of the Aiken Bar, an able attorney, to represent her.

The evidence as presented recorded that the husband's body was found buried in the back yard of the couple's home about eight months after he had disappeared, and that the wife and their child had continued to occupy the dwelling. According to her confession and other evidence, she had killed her mate and buried him at about three a. m.

The wife and her daughter testified that the husband came home about two a. m., hungry, drunk and creating a disturbance, that he abused the wife and threatened the child, whereupon the defendant in self defense seized a fire iron from the fireplace and struck him much harder than she had intended. The blow was fatal.

Jurors were told that the deceased had a history of abusing his wife on several occasions, so they found her not guilty, despite the fact that she had interred him unceremoniously.

The solicitor was much chagrined, but Attorney Surasky was highly elated.

After the trial was over, he came by the judge's office and I asked, "Bennie, how did you do it?"

He smiled and said, "Judge, my client was just like all the rest of them. She didn't know the gun was loaded."

## *Three Is One Too Many*

About ten o'clock one Saturday night I was returning to my hotel room at Hilton Head, where I was attending a lawyers meeting, when a pretty young lady called to me. "Say, Mister, would you help me for a minute?"

Somewhat astonished, especially when I observed that she was arrayed in bridal apparel, I replied, "Certainly, lady, I would be glad to help you. What would you have me do?"

This produced an unusual request. "I just got married in Greenville late this afternoon," she said, "and I want you to come to my room and take a picture of my husband carrying me over the threshold."

I obliged by taking their camera, entering their room and shooting the all-important scene as he carried her in. Then, to make sure they had a good picture, I went out on the porch, where they repeated the carrying-in performance, and made another one.

Returning their camera and chatting for a moment, I asked, "Have you ever been to Hilton Head before?" and was told this was their first trip.

In jest, I remarked, "Well, down here on Saturday night things are pretty dull. There isn't anything to do. I have the Lawrence Welk Show on the television in my room and would be delighted to have you folks join me."

The husband's sense of humor was much less than mine.

"Mister, I'm much obliged to you," he said, "but that's a problem we will just have to work out for ourselves."

I guess they did.

# EXCLAMATIONS AND EXPLANATIONS

## *Compassion And Choppers*

During a term of criminal court in Pickens County the solicitor called for trial a case charging a man named Oscar Wentway with disturbing religious worship.

He pleaded not guilty, a jury was empaneled and the pastor of the complaining Baptist church was sworn as the State's first witness. He testified that the alleged offense was committed during a revival. In a Baptist church it is customary for the choir to sing an invitational hymn at the close of the service when persons are invited to come forward and join.

The clergyman testified that while the hymn was being sung, Oscar pulled a pint bottle of whisky from his pocket, held it above his head and proceeded to prance down the aisle to where the pastor was standing. He said this conduct broke up the service and was the kind of thing he and the members could not tolerate.

I learned that Oscar was a World War I veteran, had an alcoholic problem, was unable to manage his own affairs, had $10,000 in the bank and was under control of a committee required by the Veterans Administration. When the pastor had completed his testimony, Oscar stood and announced, "Judge, I want to change my plea. I'll plead guilty. I just didn't remember this taking place, but if the preacher says that's what I did, I know that's what took place."

I accepted Oscar's plea and prepared to impose sentence. At that point, the preacher arose and said, "Judge, we don't want to make it hard on Oscar. We have nothing against him. We'd like for him to come back to the church, but we don't want him misbehaving during the service again."

This statement prompted me to inquire, "I suppose what you want me to do is put Oscar on probation."

He responded, "Yes, I suppose that's correct, Judge, if we have anything to do with it." I complied with a sentence of several months, suspended during probation.

This occurred on a Tuesday. I soon learned that my problem with Oscar was just beginning. Thursday morning, I found the probation officer waiting for me in my chambers with Oscar in his custody.

"Judge, you recall Oscar Wentway," the officer greeted me.

I admitted it. "Yes, Mr. Probation Officer. I'll never forget him as long as I live."

He then reported, "Well, last night Oscar was found drunk on the side of the road. They made a case against him of public drunkenness, and that's a violation of his probation, so we present him for such directive as you wish to issue in this case."

I was greatly concerned because of Oscar's poor mentality and was pondering what to do with him when Pickens County House Member John Gentry, a lawyer and later county judge, entered. He told me he was returning to the Legislature the coming Tuesday and offered to contact officials at the State Hospital in Columbia regarding Oscar. He proposed, "If you will commit him down there for thirty days of observation, I'll see if they will keep him."

The suggestion pleased me, because the case was one I couldn't overlook entirely, yet I was very hesitant to revoke Oscar's probation because of his mental condition. I issued an order forthwith, committing him to the State Hospital for thirty days of observation and dismissed the problem from my mind, but it wasn't long in returning. On the thirty-first day thereafter I was still holding court in the same circuit but had rotated to Greenville when the Pickens County probation officer entered the courtroom with Oscar following him. I recessed proceedings and asked the officer if I could help him.

"Yes, Your Honor," he began. "You will remember Oscar Wentway, won't you?"

I repeated my recent admission. "Yes, I remember Oscar and I'll never forget him as long as I live."

The officer restored my burden by reporting, "Well, the authorities at the State Hospital kept him for thirty days and gave him an examination, then refused to keep him any longer. They returned him to my custody, and I am bringing him back to you for such further directive as the court wishes to impose."

I looked at the culprit and said, "Oscar, I don't know what to do with you. What do you think I ought to do with you?"

Oscar flashed a big smile, revealing that he didn't have a tooth in his head, and said, "Judge, the first thing I think you ought to do is help me get my teeth back."

"That seems to be a very reasonable request," I agreed, and inquired, "Mr. Probation Officer, where are Oscar's teeth? Who has them?"

The probation officer was well posted. "Your Honor," he replied, "Oscar's teeth are in a glass of water, on a night stand by the side of his bed, in his cabin, at the foot of the mountain at Rocky Bottom, where he left them the night before he was arrested for being drunk on the side of the road."

Armed with this important information, I was then able to deal with at least one of Oscar's woes. "Let's agree on one thing," I directed. "Regardless of what we do with Oscar in the last analysis, let's agree that we will grant his request and get his teeth back."

Next I suggested, "You know, Oscar, the best thing that could happen to you would be for you to get married. You need someone to take care of you. It would be a good thing if you could go back over in Pickens, find some good woman, propose to her and make her your wife. You've got ten thousand dollars in the bank, and you could support some good woman from Pickens County."

This suggestion unwrapped another of Oscar's problems. "Judge," he said, "over there in Pickens they done talked about me so bad, won't none of 'em have me."

"I can well understand that," I admitted. "Greenville is close by, and it's a bigger town and has more unmarried women. Perhaps you could come over to Greenville and propose to some woman and get married."

Again, I misfired. Oscar again favored me with his big smile and backed further away from wedlock. "People in Pickens wouldn't like that," he said. "They always talking about you ought to patronize home industry."

Desperate, I surrendered by declaring, "Mr. Probation Officer, it's obvious that Oscar has better answers than I have questions. He has been in confinement at the State Hospital for thirty days. I will let this thirty-day period of incarceration serve as his punishment for getting drunk on the side of the road. Perhaps, by the time you catch him again, some other judge will have rotated into this circuit who is more astute than I am. Maybe he will know what to do with Oscar Wentway. I do not. But Mr. Probation Officer, be sure to get his teeth back."

## *Conditional Credibility*

It has been my observation over the years that normally a witness who comes to court endeavors to tell the truth.

But when he attempts to testify with too much precision, a jury may well question his credibility. Pitfalls are often present, for example when he is asked by a lawyer to declare distances, such as how long were the skid marks made by an automobile before the impact or collision. Most jurors do not expect testimony on such points to be exact, and a witness is better off if he sticks to estimates.

One witness was asked to estimate distances. He did so without indicating whether he was stating them in exact or estimated figures. On cross-examination he was pressed by additional questions and apparently became fearful that the jury might think he was lying.

Finally, this pressure pushed him into panic. He got his words mixed up and floundered, then in desperation delivered this outburst, "Now lawyer, don't question me any more. I'm not lying exactly, I'm just lying approximately."

## *Any Way, It Hurt*

In Bishopville I was trying a personal injury case in which the plaintiff claimed he had suffered severe leg damage. His lawyer had subpoenaed the doctor who had treated the complainant, and while testifying, the physician repeatedly referred to the affliction as sciatica.

Fearing that some of the jurors might not be familiar with sciatica, the plaintiff's attorney asked the witness, "Doctor, tell us if you will, what is sciatica?"

"It's simply pain," the doctor explained.

The lawyer wanted to know, "Well, why don't you just call it pain?"

"Well," the medic quipped, "I guess it's because you lawyers are always talking about habeas corpuses instead of calling it what it really is."

## *Dim On Dates*

Judges and lawyers often do not know what to expect when a witness is called. There are all kinds of witnesses. For example, we have expert witnesses, such as doctors and engineers. On the other hand, we get some witnesses who are woefully ignorant.

I recall one who testified in court in Dillon County. A lawyer was striving to establish by this witness the date on which an accident occurred.

He asked him, "I believe this wreck happened on the tenth of November of last year, is that correct?"

The witness' response left the matter of date entirely up in the air.

He said, "I don't understand nothing 'cept Saturday and Sunday."

## *Disappointed Defendant*

Some civil case litigants and persons charged with crime lean heavily upon their lawyers. Their evaluation of a good lawyer is one who always wins in their behalf.

For many years South Carolina judges and solicitors disposed of criminal cases without the assistance of court-appointed defense attorneys. Then along came the case of *Gideon vs. Wainwright* and others, in which it was held that almost every defendant was entitled to appointed counsel as a matter of due process. Then, adding to the burdens of lawyers and judges, the United States Supreme Court said almost in effect that every defendant is entitled to an appeal and a free court record. Subsequently, numerous post-conviction applications for release, much akin to appeals, sprouted. Allegations that defense counsel was incompetent became a frequent part of these moves by defendants who had been sentenced.

This incompetent counsel contention was among several allegations made by a prisoner who applied to me for release, and so I asked him, "Why do you say your lawyer was incompetent?"

He replied, "A good lawyer would'a sprung me."

## *A Shell-Shocked Lawyer*

Sometimes a witness will throw his lawyer in the creek, so to speak. I observed such a "toss" while holding court once in Lancaster, but it was only temporary.

We were trying a personal injury case. Testimony indicated that the injury was only negligible and that a jury award of two hundred or three hundred dollars would have been sufficient compensation.

Attorney Reese Williams was defending and Lawyer Ned Gregory represented the plaintiff.

At one point Mr. Williams asked the plaintiff, "Do you mean to tell me that on the basis of the meager showing you have made in this case that you are asking the jury to give you seven thousand five hundred dollars?"

The plaintiff answered, "No, sir."

Startled, Mr. Gregory sort of slipped down in his chair, then grabbed his complaint to check on the amount it asked for. Mr. Williams immediately checked his copy and I quickly checked the original on my desk. We all discovered that the prayer for relief was seven thousand five hundred dollars.

Mr. Williams continued his cross-examination with this question, "Well, if you're not asking this jury to give you seven thousand five hundred dollars, what are you asking the jury to give you?"

The witness clarified his position by responding, "I don't want the jury to give me anything. I want the defendant to pay it."

Greatly relieved, Mr. Gregory regained his shattered composure and the trial continued.

## *No Traveling Woman*

As a judge tours the state to try cases, he hears many unusual expressions.

Once I asked a defendant how much whisky he had drunk at the time a fight took place.

He replied, "I don't know exactly, but I think it was a pretty good much."

In another case, a "Low Country" woman was testifying when she was asked where she was on a specific day when a crime was alleged to have occurred.

"I was at home where I should'a been," she indignantly replied.

Then she turned, looked at me and assured, "Judge, I ain't one of them traveling women."

## *Milking A Dry Cow*

Some lawyers injure their client's case by excessive cross-examination. This also can bore jurors and produce undesirable testimony.

One lawyer in a case before me cross-examined a witness so lengthily and repetitiously that when he finally finished, I declared a recess in order to give myself and the weary jurors a rest.

Soon thereafter, the bailiff approached me in chambers and said, "Judge, do you know what one of those jurors said about the lawyer who over-examined a witness?"

I answered, "No. What did he say?"

"He said," the bailiff divulged, "That lawyer is the kind'a fellow what if he was a dairyman he would keep on milking a cow after she had gone dry."

## *End To Ecstasy*

While I was trying money damage claims in a lower South Carolina county, Attorney Mortimer Weinberg, Sr. was representing a defendant and the insurance company which had the liability coverage.

The claim involved a plaintiff about twenty-two years of age and married. He was seriously injured by a fall. Among the allegations of the complaint was one that he had been made impotent by the injury. A urologist, testifying for the plaintiff, so stated from the witness stand.

Mr. Weinberg was one of the most delightful men I have ever had in court. He spoke with a distinct Southern drawl, never became excited, and always represented his clients well. In cross-examining the urologist, he sought to further pursue the impotency issue.

He asked the witness, "Doctor, just tell the jury, if you will, about how often does a man have sexual relations anyhow."

The urologist responded, "Well, Mr. Weinberg, that's a question that is pretty difficult to answer. I don't know that I could give you an answer with any real accuracy."

Mr. Weinberg began trying to pinpoint this frequency of male ability. "But even so," he persisted, "Doctor, you have come here as an expert. Certainly you can give this jury some idea about a thing like this. It may be important in the trial of this case."

The witness hedged by replying, "Well, Mr. Weinberg, it just depends on so many things that it makes the question very difficult to answer."

"But, doctor," the veteran and skillful attorney further persisted, "just take an average, ordinary man, about how many times a week or a month would he have sexual relations?"

Each time the question was put, the courtroom crowd became quieter. Perhaps every man there wanted to measure his grain by the other fellow's half-bushel.

The doctor continued, still in a vague vein: "Well, it just depends on a lot of things, like the inclination of one's partner and his state of health. And then, there is a psychological factor which is involved."

Mr. Weinberg stubbornly held his ground and continued to slowly advance.

"Certainly," he insisted, "you can give us some idea. Just take an ordinary man and give us an estimate, if you can't testify with any accuracy."

Mr. Weinberg, about sixty-five and balding, awaited the answer.

Finally, the urologist ventured more into details.

"Mr. Weinberg," he said, "for example, take a man between twenty and thirty years of age—for him it might be a number of times; take a man between thirty and forty, it would be a different number, a smaller number, if you please; and between forty and fifty the number would change again, still a little smaller, Mr. Weinberg. And between fifty and sixty, the number would get even smaller. And then, Mr. Weinberg"—and here the doctor wearily waved his hands and sadly concluded—"it just dwindles out."

The courtroom crowd was as still as a desert with no wind—that is until Mr. Weinberg moaned, "Doctor, you have broken my heart!"

## *Understanding Pays*

It is not unusual for some persons who are unaccustomed to courtrooms and their crowds and procedures to become frightened at the very thought of having to testify in the trial of a case. To such witnesses, the entire experience is dreaded as an ordeal.

Some lawyers have acquired the art of approaching them gently and tactfully guiding them into a state of ease and composure. In Greenville, Attorney Harold Morris called a badly frightened young woman to the witness stand. It was immediately apparent that she was about to make a very poor witness because she was so emotionally upset. Mr. Morris, realizing her predicament and the effect it could have on her testimony and his case, elected to quiet her nerves and get them both on common ground.

"Young lady, are you frightened?" he kindly asked.

"Yes, actually I am," she admitted.

"I can well understand that," he told her. "Just to tell you the truth, I'm a little bit afraid myself."

This did the trick. They settled into a fruitful question-and-answer exchange, and she made him and his client a good witness.

## *He Told It His Way*

Most witnesses in court confine their answers to questions asked by the lawyers, but occasionally we encounter a witness who, if you ask him what time it is, will tell you how to make a watch. One of these rare blabbermouths took the witness stand while I was trying a wreck case in Columbia.

The gist of the suit was that a man and his son were test-driving a car off a used car lot in Columbia when it was involved in a collision. The driver of the other car was suing the man and his son and the used car dealer. When the elder of the two car testers took the stand, the examining attorney unwittingly opened wide the door to loquaciousness with this, as he thought, routine inquiry, "I believe you were in the automobile with your son the day this collision happened."

Forthwith, Dad proceeded to avalanche the court, as follows: "Yes, sir, lawyer. I tell you how it was. You know me and my boy live over at Olympia Mill. My old lady lives there, too. We been married thirty-seven years and been living in the same house for nineteen years.

"Well, I been working on the first shift that day and when I got off about two o'clock, I said to the boy, 'Let's me and you go to town.' We didn't have no automobile, so we went down to the curb and caught a bus. Rode up town and got off the bus and just started walking down the street. We come to this used car lot. My boy said, 'Pa, we ought to get us a used car.' I said, 'Son, we ain't got no money to buy a used car. What we gonna use for money?' He said, 'Well, we can pawn the television set and get a down payment and we just sign for the rest of it.' "

Warming up, the untiring witness continued:

"He [the son] said, 'Come on in here, Pa, and let's look at some of these automobiles and see if we can't buy one.' So I said, 'All right son, I ain't got nothing else to do. We can look around and we don't have to buy nohow.' And so we looked around and finally we found a green Mercury. It just really appealed to my boy."

At this point, he left the mainstream of his narration, pointed to a nearby courtroom seat occupant and proudly exclaimed, "That's my boy sitting there on the front row. Ain't he about as bald-headed as anybody you ever saw?"

Having dispensed with this edification of the audience, he prolifically plunged into the next chapter of his detailing:

"And so we called the man that runs the place and told him that we wanted to look at that green Mercury. He said, 'It's a mighty fine automobile. Why don't you just get in it and try it out? You don't have to buy it if you don't like it. Get in and drive it.' We got in and it didn't have no gasoline in it. So I told the man it looked like it was setting on zero. And he said, 'Well, take this slip of paper and go to the Gulf station over there across the street.'

"We went across there to the Gulf station and put two gallons in it and me and the boy started down the street and got to this intersection. Now, that's just exactly the way it happened. That's where we had the collision. I'm here to tell the truth and I ain't gonna lie for nobody."

Finally finished, he turned to me and said, "A fellow comes into court, he ought'a always tell the truth. Ain't that right, Cap?"

If we drew many witnesses like "Pa," we'd be trying only one case per term.

## *Sabbath At The Crossing*

I always enjoyed trying cases with Attorney Shepard Nash of Sumter.

His friends got a good laugh at him and with him in court one day. He had brought an action in behalf of a client who had been injured at a railroad crossing on Sunday.

Testimony disclosed that railroad company adjusters had gone to the scene of the crash near Sumter and had interviewed quite a few witnesses on the same Sunday the accident had happened.

Mr. Nash, in an effort to appeal to the church people on the jury, asked the first witness for the railroad company, on cross-examination, "When was it this adjuster came and talked with you about this case?"

He replied, "It was on that same Sunday."

Mr. Nash observed, "Yes, sir, out there working on the Sabbath, wasn't he? He wasn't in church where he should have been."

The second witness was called. He, too, said he had been interviewed by the adjuster on Sunday. Cross-examining, Mr. Nash again emphasized, "You say he was out there on the

Sabbath when he ought to have been in church?" Again he received an affirmative answer.

Railroad witness number three also testified that the adjuster had interviewed him on Sunday about the accident.

At this point, Mr. Nash self-righteously observed: "This adjuster should have been in church but he wasn't. He was out there working up this case against my client on the Sabbath, wasn't he?" The witness confirmed.

The railroad's next witness was called and testified.

"Where do you live?" Mr. Nash began.

The witness promptly responded, "Mr. Nash, you ought to know where I live. When this accident happened, you parked your car in my front yard that Sunday."

## *Rapid Wallowing*

Unusual words sometimes crop up in court, especially if a witness is a country fellow.

This incident had to do with rapid rolling to escape disaster.

For a little background—since few mules and horses remain on farms nowadays, moderns are not familiar with the vintage rural word, "wallow." It comes from the habit of a horse or mule to lie down and roll over and over on the ground as soon as he is freed of harness at the end of his working day. After he treats one side to this pleasurable massaging, he often will turn over and "wallow" on the other side. Seldom is the word used except in reference to horses and mules.

I was trying a case in Aiken wherein a man claimed a tractor almost ran over him and knocked him to the ground. He said he escaped being struck by the tractor but was injured when he purposely rolled into a ditch. His claim for damages was not large, but he was vigorously pushing it in court.

"How did you get out of the way of the tractor?" his lawyer asked him. "Looks like it would have hit you. How did you escape?"

The plaintiff was quick on the draw.

"I had to wallow fast," he said.

# CONFABBING WITH THE JUDGE

## *Polishing A Plea*

For several years Fred Thompson was my barber in the Montgomery Building in Spartanburg. The shine man there was named Elvis West. He was the only fellow I've ever known who served in the Army by mistake.

When the draft came along, Elvis decided not to register and see what happened. Several months later he received one of those well known "Greetings" cards from the President, directing him to report to the draft board for examination. Even though he had not registered, he received the card because there was another Elvis West in Spartanburg, and the card was actually meant for him instead of the shine boy.

Elvis reasoned that the officials had caught him anyway, in spite of his failure to register. Thirty-nine months later the mistake was discovered, but by then it was long too late for my friend to keep out of uniform.

Anyway, Elvis was out of the Army and happily back in civilian life and at his old trade. One day I treated myself to a haircut and a shoe shine at the same time.

After Mr. Thompson finished cutting my hair, I turned to Elvis and gave him a nickel—in fun, because I knew there was nothing left in the world like a five-cent shoe shine. By then the price had gone up to fifteen or twenty cents.

As I started to leave and had my hand on the door knob, I queried Elvis, "The amount I gave you was correct, wasn't it?"

He bowed and scraped and assured me, "Yes, sir, Judge; yes, sir, Judge," and reminded me, "My case may be coming up any day now. That's quite all right."

I reached into my pocket for more money, as I had intended to do before Elvis broached his pending criminal court appearance, and admonished him, "Elvis, let me tell you something. You're not going to bribe a circuit judge with ten or fifteen cents worth of shoe shine."

But he insisted, "Judge, you're shore welcome to it. And if you want to change your mind, you can still just keep it."

## *Cash Ain't Comical*

Some defendants just seem to fare poorly in court, especially when a jury makes the determination. Some of them are taxicab drivers.

Attorney J. R. "Coot" Flynn was trying a damage case before me in Union. The action stemmed from this situation: a taxicab and a bicycle being ridden by a small boy were involved in a slight collision, actually a "brush-off" contact. The lad fell off, jumped to his feet crying and ran home. The bicycle was damaged about two or three dollars' worth. There was a serious question whether the rider had been injured at all, but his parents sued the taxi company for ten thousand dollars.

Mr. Flynn was very effective before both civil and criminal court juries, so in this case he wound up with a verdict of some four thousand four hundred dollars, making it one of the few instances where I felt compelled to reduce the verdict or grant a new trial. In an effort to put a compromise value on the case, I reduced the verdict by half, thereby granting a new trial unless the plaintiffs agreed to cut the award to two thousand two hundred dollars. Actually, in my personal opinion, that amount was too large, but I realized that if the case were tried again, Mr. Flynn might persuade the jury to award four thousand four hundred dollars or even five thousand five hundred or six thousand six hundred dollars. My decision didn't satisfy either side. Both appealed.

A year or so of futile settlement negotiations ensued before the two thousand two hundred dollar award I had suggested was mutually accepted. Later, Mr. Flynn came to my office with a petition asking me to approve his fee at one-third of the settlement figure.

I told him, "Mr. Flynn, I would be delighted to approve the fee of one-third. As a matter of fact, I think you ought to get a half."

"Judge," he asked, "why do you say that?"

I replied, "Mr. Flynn, I said that because I think you were hurt just as bad as the boy was."

"Coot" laughed, then said, "Judge, don't tease me about money. When dollar bills are involved, I haven't got much sense of humor."

## *Amateur's Approval*

As I traveled South Carolina holding courts as a circuit judge, I encountered quite a few bailiffs. Many of them were rather interesting characters, and most of them were always anxious to be of help. However, sometimes a sheriff or other appointing authority was inclined to appoint men who were old or disabled and could not be of much assistance to the court.

As a result, unusual incidents sometimes occurred, as once in Charleston, when I heard a motion for a directed verdict at the close of testimony.

Counsel for the defendant made the motion and sat on my left. The plaintiff's attorney was seated at my right. A bailiff sat near the desk of the plaintiff's lawyer.

After the motion had been stated, I looked toward the plaintiff's counsel's table and inquired, "What do you say to that?"

The bailiff, thinking I was looking at and speaking to him, responded.

"Judge, it's all right with me."

## *Grading Grounds Differ*

In 1958 while holding court in Columbia, I became involved in legal conflict between two attorney friends, Carlisle Roberts for the defendant and Monroe Fulmer for the plaintiff. Their courtroom controversy produced a very interesting side development dating back to law school days.

Mr. Roberts had attacked the validity of Mr. Fulmer's pleadings. He contended that the case should be dismissed because the complaint did not state a cause of action.

Friend Roberts had taught me at the University of South Carolina Law School. A few years later he left the faculty and entered the practice of law in Columbia. When arguments had been completed, I told him, "Mr. Roberts, the first time I was reversed by the State Supreme Court was because I made a decision in favor of Neville Holcombe's client and Neville was my first law teacher. He taught a pre-law course at Wofford College, and I took that course before entering law school. I guess one of the reasons I decided in favor of my former law teacher, Mr. Holcombe, was that I felt he would cite me good law. Now, I don't want to get reversed again."

Mr. Roberts assured me that if I would decide the case in the favor of his client he would see that my decision was affirmed by the Supreme Court.

This prompted Mr. Fulmer, equal to the situation, to cite and declare:

"Your Honor, I too studied at the feet of fatherly Professor Carlisle Roberts. He has attacked the validity of my papers. He says my complaint is not good. It was all right for him to grade my papers at the law school, but I don't want him grading my papers here in the Richland County Courthouse."

## *Ruling Unacceptable*

I was holding civil court in Greenwood during the early 1960s when Francis Nicholson, who later became resident judge of the Eighth Judicial Circuit, appeared before me, representing a woman who had brought an action against an insurance company concerning a policy dispute.

As the trial proceeded, it developed that the plaintiff had not proven her case, so I threw it out of court by directing a verdict for the defendant.

The woman was much disturbed by this disposition. About six the next morning she telephoned me at the motel where I was staying and complained, "Judge, I don't understand what happened in court over there yesterday. I am sure I had a good claim against the insurance company. I just don't understand how you could end it by doing a thing like that."

I patiently told her, as I have told hundreds of others who attempt to talk to the judge about a case which is in court or has been in court, "Lady, you have a good lawyer. You go and talk to him. I am sure he will explain it to you. That's where you ought to get your advice."

But she didn't appear to be convinced. "Judge, I've already talked to my good lawyer", she said. "But he doesn't understand it either."

### *Elusive Courtroom*

When I first went to Allendale to try circuit court cases, former Governor Robert McNair was still practicing law in that town. He enjoys relating this incident about my initial judicial experience there.

Allendale is not a large town. Normally, when I went to county seats of this size, I could easily spot the courthouse and didn't have to ask anyone for directions, because the courthouse in such places is usually the big brick building in the downtown area.

When I arrived in Allendale, I mistakenly got onto a side street and lost my bearings. While wondering which way to turn, I saw two men shoveling dirt in a ditch beside the street, so I stopped my car to inquire for directions.

"Hey, fellows," I hailed them. "Could you tell me how to get to the courthouse?"

They sized me up skeptically and one asked, "Mister, are you a police?"

Hoping to impress them and to make sure I was given the correct information, I replied, "No, I'm not a police. I'm a judge."

Duly impressed, they gave me directions.

As I turned away, I overheard one of them remark to the other, "What kind of judge air he? 'Don't even know where the courthouse is!".

## *Invitation Loaded*

Luke Williamson of Aiken and I were fellow students at the University of South Carolina Law School.

When I became a circuit judge and went to Aiken to try cases, he was a circuit solicitor and I had the pleasure of working with him. He was energetic and diligent and worked hard as a prosecutor. He knew that some defendants came to court in a mood to plead guilty, and he always sought to get their pleas rolling as rapidly as possible.

Late Monday afternoon near recess time, he faced the audience and spoke in formal fashion, "Be there a man present today who would like to enter a guilty plea, let him come forward at this time."

Nobody made a move, so the solicitor, addressing the court, reported, "Your Honor, I find no takers."

Unable to resist the temptation, I suggested, "Mr. Solicitor, perhaps it is because you don't have a very inviting proposition."

## *The Job Was Open*

Around 1966 Roger Milliken, a well-known textile manufacturer with headquarters at Spartanburg, decided to merge seven plants into one. Approximately seventy-seven million dollars' worth of stock was involved in all of the companies combined.

In such cases, those who propose to merge offer stockholders of the respective companies a stipulated amount of stock in the new corporation. If the stockholders accept this stock there is no dispute, but in this case stockholders owning about three million dollars' worth of shares did not like the merger terms and decided to contest it.

I was the resident circuit judge at Spartanburg at the time. L. A. Odom of the Spartanburg Bar came to my office. He was among attorneys representing the Milliken interests. He asked me to set a hearing on a petition to appoint a board of three men to appraise the stock of the dissenting shareholders. This was an important proceeding, since the board I was to appoint would make the appraisal and sit much like a jury.

Somewhat facetiously, I told Mr. Odom, "I am not at all sure but what I ought to disqualify myself in this case."

He wanted to know why. I explained, "Well, you know that among those plants which are to be merged is the Pacolet Manufacturing Co. And, L. A., about thirty-three years ago, between my freshman and sophomore years at Wofford College, I went down to Pacolet Mills—it was during the depression—and applied for a job. They took my application and I haven't heard from them yet. It might be that I am agitated with them for not giving me the job, or at least letting me know what they did with my application."

Mr. Odom, well-known for his good sense of humor as well as for his outstanding legal ability, was amused. "Judge," he said, "I hope you don't misunderstand the situation. I can guarantee you that your application has not been turned down, and if you still want the job, I certainly can get it for you now."

## *Clever Communicating*

Miss Folsom Smith of Spartanburg was my very efficient circuit court reporter for seventeen years, from 1949 until I went to the State Supreme Court in 1967.

Previously, she was my secretary when I was Speaker of the House, and before that she was administrative secretary to Governor Strom Thurmond at the State House. She also had served as secretary to the attorney for the Land Bank in Columbia. So when she came to Spartanburg, she brought with her a gold mine of experience, a keen understanding of human nature and the answers to many questions.

As circuit judge, I was away from Spartanburg during the week for most of the year. On Saturdays, Miss Folsom and I would work at Spartanburg Courthouse on correspondence and orders and hold hearings. It was routine for her to open my mail before I arrived at the office.

After I had held my first court in Columbia, Dave Robinson, one of the state's leading attorneys, wrote me a letter congratulating me upon conducting a very successful term of court on my first visit to his town.

Upon my arrival at the office, Miss Folsom read the letter to me and commented that Mr. Robinson was one of the smartest lawyers in the state.

I agreed with her and then remarked in good humor, "At the same time, Miss Folsom, won't you agree that a lawyer doesn't have to be smart to know that I am a good judge?"

Quick on the trigger, she replied, "Oh, yes, even a dumb lawyer would know that you are an extraordinarily fine judge, but only the smart ones would know to write you a letter about it."

## *Service Beyond The Call Of Duty*

Charleston was one of the first counties in South Carolina where juries began awarding what may be called "large" verdicts in personal injury cases. Over the years, my observation has been that increasingly juries have been inclined to make such verdicts substantial and sometimes larger than their awards in death cases.

Buist Rivers, an outstanding Charleston attorney, specialized in defending actions against insurance companies, many of them personal injury cases.

Once while I was holding court in Charleston, the verdicts had become so large and out of proportion—at least in the view of defense counsel—that Mr. Rivers went on the warpath outside the courthouse. He addressed civic clubs and other groups, assailing and deploring the big verdicts practice.

Among the repercussions was a local newspaper editorial entitled "Robbery in Court." Some of the lawyers wanted me to talk to the Grand Jury about this and fuss at the editor. This I would never do.

After Mr. Rivers made one of his highly persuasive speeches to a Charleston civic club, the clerk of court received a letter from one of its members who had heard the speech. He stated to the clerk that he wanted to do something about the deplorable verdict situation in Charleston County. He volunteered his services and told the clerk to place his name on the jury list so that he could come and help to straighten out the situation. This was, of course, ridiculous, because the law does not permit anyone to volunteer for jury service. Juries must be drawn "out of the hat," making the selection purely a matter of lot and, in effect, a game of chance.

Lloyd Fleming, the very efficient clerk of court, brought the letter to me, laughing, and inquired, "Judge, what must a clerk do about a letter like this?"

I told him, "Lloyd, if you want to write a letter just as ridiculous as his, you might tell him that he cannot render jury service in general, that he will have to specify which case he wants to act upon and whether he is for the plaintiff or the defendant—and that he will have to be fair about it."

## *Clipping Contact*

Understandably, lawyers like to "court" jurors.

Of course, they can't indulge in this hopefully beneficial "bouqueting" when courts are in session, other than to flavor their pre-deliberation arguments with a bit of flattery as circumstances occasionally may permit.

But before courts are convened, extracurricular friendly and attentive actions and cordiality have been known to flower.

A barber on the jury in Bennettsville, where I was holding court, supplied an appropriate "Exhibit A" in this respect. There as elsewhere in South Carolina, jury lists are made-up and publicized about ten days before the opening of court.

I was chatting with this barber after the term had been adjourned and he good naturedly told me, "Judge, I don't think my lawyer friend had any ulterior motives, but between the time they drew my name for jury service and the time court met, he came into my shop and got his hair cut four times."

## *Mistaken Identities*

Anyone who serves as a juror can usually remember the name of the presiding judge. Often the juror has only one new face to remember.

On the other hand, a presiding judge is often confronted with many people who serve as jurors or appear in court in other capacities. Judges rarely get around to individual introductions to jurors and seldom learn their names. I have been embarrassed many times to have former jurors call me "Judge Littlejohn" and apparently expect me to remember them, even though I was never introduced personally.

At one of J. G. (Dick) Floyd's barbecue celebrations on the Fourth of July, I experienced one of these embarrassments—but it was short-lived.

Dick Floyd usually invited several hundred people to his barbecue lunch. It was an annual reunion for his guests, and I would often see persons there whom I had not seen since the previous Fourth of July.

At one of these festive affairs a former juror came to me and began talking as though we were long-lost friends. It appeared that he knew me, but I couldn't recall his face or remember his name. He proceeded to talk about things with which I was supposed to be familiar. I didn't want to admit that I didn't recognize him, so I contented myself with carrying on a lot of small talk, like bragging on the barbecue and commenting on the weather.

Finally, a friend of his walked up and he proceeded to introduce his friend to me.

"Mr. Wilson," he said to the new arrival, "I want you to meet my good personal friend, Judge Charles M. Pace."

My embarrassment vanished when it became apparent that my "long-lost friend" didn't know his "good personal friend" either.

## *Seated In Stratosphere*

Lawyers have a saying that if one of them loses a case he has twenty-four hours in which to cuss out the responsible judge without being held in contempt of court. A judicial friend of mine told me this story about an attorney who lost a case before him:

The judge issued a rather meaningful order involving a large amount of money. The losing lawyer was greatly upset and went to a bar that night to drown his despair. After he had consumed a sufficient number of "courage" drinks, he telephoned the judge to voice his protest and position. He told His Honor that his order was drastic and exceeded the jurisdiction of the court. Then, indignantly, he asked the judge, "Who do you think you are anyhow? God?"

The judge was equal to the situation. "Talk a little louder," he suggested. "I can't hear you well. You must be calling from down on earth."

## *No Middle Man*

Traveling into South Carolina's forty-six counties during the some seventeen years I was a circuit judge required a lot of restaurant eating. Courts create news in small towns much more than they do in the cities, and just about everybody is aware when the courts are in session, although many of the folks aren't directly involved.

Around noon on the opening day of a Walterboro term, I drove to a restaurant on the edge of town for lunch.

Over the years I would often ask restaurant waitresses, "Who is the best lawyer in town?" Many of their answers were amusing.

So, as I prepared to give my order in the Walterboro restaurant, I asked the waitress ( who I didn't think knew me, because I'd only been in town about two hours ), "Young lady, if you were in some serious trouble in this town and needed a good lawyer quickly, who would you go to see?"

She was strictly on the ball. "I wouldn't fiddle with a lawyer at all," she said. "I'd come straight to you and cut out the middle man."

## *He Had It*

In South Carolina jurors once were drawn by a youngster approved by the court and called "the jury boy."

These juvenile "officers of the court" were mostly boys, although occasionally a girl was given the job. Their task was simply to reach inside a receptacle, pick up a slip of paper bearing a prospective juror's name, and hand it to the clerk of court until the trial panel being drawn was completed.

Once while holding court in Abbeville, I used part of my lunch hour for a walk and strolled into a nearby residential section. At one house, a lad about seven or eight years of age hailed me, "Say, Mister, aren't you the judge?"

I acknowledged that I was and asked him, "How did you know I am the judge?"

"When you were here about two months ago, I was the jury boy," he reminded me.

"That's mighty fine," I commended him. "Would you like to come back and serve as jury boy again?"

"No, sir", he replied.

Curious, I inquired further. "I'd be interested to know why you wouldn't want to be the jury boy again."

He said, "Judge, that work's too hard."

## *The D. A. Dug This*

Once I went fishing down on the Santee-Cooper near Moncks Corner. While we were at a fish camp, the operator—named Green—learned I was a judge and came to me with a personal problem. He had received a government questionnaire directed toward his possible selection for Federal Court jury service. These questionnaires ask recipients to state their age, occupation and other personal background information, apparently endeavoring to assure a representative cross-section assortment of jurors.

Mr. Green's questionnaire was puzzling and worrying him considerably. He just didn't know what to do with it. He said he didn't want to serve and wondered what would happen to him, contempt of court or possibly otherwise, if he ignored the paper.

I decided to help him out of his predicament. I told him to disregard all the questions and blank spaces on the questionnaire and to take his pencil and write across the face of it simply these words, "I ain't never in favor of convicting nobody of nothing no time."

He eagerly and quickly did this.

A year or so later when I returned to the camp, I asked him if he had been called to serve. He assured me he had heard nothing more from the questionnaire since he mailed it back—and I'm certain he hadn't.

## *Financially Motivated*

In the spring of 1968, while President Lyndon Johnson was still in office, he announced on a Sunday night that he definitely would not be a candidate for re-election.

The following morning, while I was having my car gassed up, I asked the service station attendant, "What do you think about President Johnson not seeking re-election?"

Apparently he figured that finances, not politics, were involved, and reasoned, "Judge, he must have something better in mind or he wouldn't give up such a good paying job."

## *Feeding The "Fixings"*

Several years ago I was returning from a Judges Conference in Montreal and was in flight to New York when I struck up a conversation with my seat companion. It developed that he was an attorney who practiced tax law part-time in Washington and taught in the law school at one of the universities.

During our conversation he commented that he was returning to New York for a conference with the IBM people. He said that they were working on a computer into which one could feed evidence, push the right buttons, and find out what a jury would do in a particular case.

I was aware of the fact that computers do amazing things. I decided to pursue the matter a little further by asking him, "What would happen if some jurors were fixed on one side, or for that matter on both sides? There are places where that goes on a great deal."

This didn't seem to faze him at all. "That would cause no problem," he informed me. "We would just feed that into the computer along with the evidence."

## *He Didn't Like It*

Stokes Houck, who practiced law in Florence, was one of the state's outstanding attorneys. He defended many cases in Florence and adjoining counties, and I always enjoyed having him in court.

I went to Bennettsville to hold court, and Stokes came over from Florence to defend a railroad company in a lawsuit. It is not unusual in a small county for most of the local lawyers to be employed on the plaintiff's side, and an attorney from another county is sometimes placed in a rather difficult position to defend.

This case was hard-fought and ended with a substantial verdict for damages. Mr. Houck normally accepted his defeats calmly, but the verdict jarred him and he became slightly upset.

When the verdict was reported in, I asked the clerk to exhibit it to the court and show it to the lawyers for the plaintiff and defendant. I noted there was something irregular about it and inquired, "Is there any objection to the form of the verdict?" Plaintiff's counsel quickly assured me there was no such objection.

I next queried defense counsel, "What do you say, Mr. Houck?"

It transpired that he had plenty to say.

He rose immediately, raised his hands above his head, pounded on his desk and wrathfully exclaimed: "Yes, sir, I object to the form of the verdict; I object to the contents of the verdict; I object to the paper that it's written on; I object to everything about it, and I want the record to so show."

## *Littlejohn And Larceny*

From the story of Robin Hood it will be recalled that one of his right-hand men was a fellow named Littlejohn, and that Robin and his crew were noted for taking from the rich and giving to the poor. That's how the legend goes.

I once tried a civil case in which the jury awarded a rather substantial amount. Judges frequently must hear new trial and judgment motions after a verdict has been returned. Accordingly, the lawyer for the defendant in this case made the conventional motions. I thought the question had properly been one for the jury and let the verdict stand.

Later that day, the clerk of court remarked to me, "Judge, you'll be interested in knowing what the lawyer for the defendant said about you out in the hallway before he went home."

"Mr. Clerk, go ahead and tell me about it," I requested.

He then informed me, "Judge, the lawyer said that even as in the days of Robin Hood, Littlejohn is still taking from the rich and giving to the poor."

## *Progress Ain't Always Progress*

There are a few oldtimers left in the world who contend that everything they used to make was better than anything being produced in these modern times. For instance, there is the fellow who buys a magnificent latest model automobile and claims it isn't as good as the pre-World War II models.

This fault-finding surfaced in a case before me in court one time. The alcoholic involved presented a sentencing problem, so I questioned him, including this query, "Why do you drink so much liquor?"

He was all set with an answer. "Judge," he said, "I guess it's because they ain't making water like they used to."

# IN AND ABOUT THE TRIAL COURT

## *Don't Get Too Involved*

When I was holding court in Sumter, one of the outstanding attorneys there was Mortimer Weinberg, Sr. Mortimer enjoyed a splendid practice, mostly defending insurance companies in wreck cases.

One day a truck from Connecticut was proceeding through South Carolina along Highway 15, which passes through Sumter County. The name on the truck's side was "The Great Silver Fleet Van Lines." I learned as the trial progressed that "The Great Silver Fleet Van Lines" was actually one truck and one driver and that the driver owned the truck, thereby making him and his rig the entire operation. At the time of the accident, he was traveling from Connecticut to Florida and his only cargo in the large carrier was a boat he was supposed to deliver in Miami.

He had come from Connecticut to participate in the trial of the case, and Mr. Weinberg was representing the insurance company for "The Great Silver Fleet Van Lines."

The driver was very nonchalant about the entire affair. He was insulated by a very good insurance policy, he wasn't going to have to pay any damages himself, and so he did not greatly concern himself with the trial. He appeared reluctant to become deeply involved in the litigation, so he testified a little on one side and then shifted his testimony to the other side.

A verdict for the plaintiff was returned against him.

A few days later I saw a letter Mr. Weinberg had written to his insurance company client. He reported what had transpired at the trial, enumerated what various people had testified to, and related what the jury had done. He even gave a short summary of what each defense witness had said on the witness stand.

But when his report referred to the truck driver, this is all he said:

"I recommend that this man confine his activities to driving a truck. He would have a hard time making a living as a witness."

### *Snoozing Was Safer*

When a case is appealed to the Supreme Court, its record in the lower court is printed. Entries in this record often include testimony and the judge's charge to the trial jury.

Once the loser in a wreck case I had tried in Camden as circuit judge appealed, and the typed record of the lower case proceeding was brought to me. In reading my charge, I discovered that I had defined "negligence" and "willfulness" to the jury.

This wasn't all I found.

Right in between the two definitions, the words, "Shake him again," stared at me. Counsel presenting the record requested an explanation.

Fortunately, I remembered in detail that this had taken place: Amid my charge, I had discovered that the third juror on the front row was asleep. I paused as though I was about to reprimand him, when the juror beside him shook him and woke him up. I proceeded with my charge and had just defined "negligence," when I glanced at the jury box and discovered that the drowsy juror was asleep again. In an aside remark, I asked the juror who had shaken him before to "Shake him again," and these words became part of the record.

His companion re-shook him, but it didn't work. Two definitions later, I discovered he was asleep again. I decided he might do less harm asleep than if he were awake, so I let him finish his nap while I completed my charge.

## *Next*

Judicial expediting of cases in an effort to clear dockets isn't always easy.

Some judges "push the docket," so to speak, and frequently save taxpayers the expense of one or two days of court. Others let the lawyers, solicitor and other attachés "set the pace." I was among the circuit judges who attempted to process a maximum number of cases in a minimum number of days. I did this by alerting attorneys and witnesses in the next two pending cases while trying another. This kept one trial going while two sets of lawyers and their clients were awaiting in the wings.

During a term of court in Sumter, we were running in high gear by getting cases lined up for action while one was being tried. I kept the jury in the courtroom all week as part of the docket-clearing effort.

Reacting to this pressure, a lawyer told a bailiff, "Judge Littlejohn runs his court just like a barber shop. When he finishes trying one case, he hollers 'Next!' "

## *Mechanical Tutoring*

Court reporters take down testimony variously. Some use shorthand, some a stenotype machine, some a stenomask and others employ a recording machine.

When I went to Abbeville to hold court, some of the lawyers told me about the time a reporter used a stenotype machine for the first time in court there.

One of the bailiffs had never seen such a machine before. He was unable to read or write. The machine fascinated him, so he asked a lawyer what it was and was told that the reporter was mechanically recording the court proceedings.

"I believe I'll buy me one of them machines, 'cause I can't read and write with a pencil."

## *Barter Southern Style*

Attorney E. W. Cantwell had a strong following in Williamsburg County, of which Kingstree is the county seat. His supporters elected him to the State Senate. While he was serving, the Legislature voted its members an expense item commonly called "extra pay," as had been customary over the years. However, a lawsuit was brought to recover the money from each member, alleging that it was additional compensation unauthorized by law.

A special Supreme Court held that the disbursement was unconstitutional. Accordingly, legislators who had drawn the $700 expense item for the previous year were required to refund same, and most of them did so, voluntarily. J. M. Daniels, then state attorney general, brought an action to recover $700 each from several holdouts, including Mr. Cantwell, who refused to play ball. Instead, he filed an answer in his own behalf, in which he not only declared that the state was not entitled to recover from him but owed him some $5,800 for services over and above the call of duty of the average senator.

Circuit Judge William H. Grimball of Charleston, sitting in Kingstree, heard a demurrer to the counterclaim and answer. He sustained the state's demurrer and did not permit Mr. Cantwell to answer. When I rotated into that circuit in the fall of 1950, Hoke Robinson, then an assistant attorney general, came to Kingstree and moved for judgment on the grounds that no answer was filed and the state was entitled to recover. After hearing Robinson's motion, I invited Mr. Cantwell to state his position, even though he was in default.

He responded, "Your Honor, my position in this matter is that I want a Williamsburg County jury to pass on this matter. It's a matter a jury ought to decide. Not only that, but there is in my family seven thousand five hundred dollars worth of Confederate money issued by the State of South Carolina, and I want to use it as an offset against this seven hundred dollars."

## *Just Like Solomon*

Bailiffs usually are good politicians before they receive their appointments. Those who aren't at the beginning soon learn the tricks of the trade. They realize that it is to their advantage to stand in with "the courthouse ring" and members of the bar.

I had held circuit courts in Winnsboro on several occasions. One spring morning I returned and parked my car in the space designated for the presiding judge. When I arrived, Allen Mitchell, an excellent bailiff who also preached some on the side, came to my car to assist me in carrying my briefcase and other items necessary to the operation of the court. After we had exchanged greetings, I asked Allen, "Who's the best lawyer in Winnsboro at this time?"

At that time there were only five, George Coleman, John Martin, Tom McDonald, Norwood O'Bear and Moultrie Douglas. All of them were good friends of Allen and he wasn't about to get caught in a bind by answering my question.

And so he responded, "Judge, they is all good. I would say it's about fifty-fifty any which-a-way you look at 'em."

## *Monkeying Misfires*

A few days before I was to hold a term of criminal court in Kingstree, I read in a newspaper that a group of young men there had formed a Ku Klux Klan of their own and had beaten up a local citizen.

When the case was called before me for trial, it developed that eight local youths were charged with assault and battery upon a ninth person. One of them pled guilty and agreed to give evidence for the State. The other seven pled not guilty and demanded a trial.

The one who turned State's evidence testified to this effect: "We procured some bedsheets and pillow cases. We wrapped the sheets around our bodies and put the pillow cases over our heads after having cut eye, nose and mouth holes in them. Then we went out on the edge of the town and took some big switches about half as big as a broom handle and got this fellow out of bed and gave him a good thrashing. Then we turned him loose and left."

Examining, the solicitor said, "Now, Mr. Witness, just tell us why you picked out this young man and decided that you were going to give him a whipping."

The witness replied, "Well, we heered he had been monkeying around."

Curious, the solicitor directed, "Just tell the jury what you mean by 'monkeying around.' "

The witness obliged with, "Aw, you know, Mr. Solicitor. Like when one monkey monkeys with another monkey's monkey."

## *Dad Was Discerning*

My father used to say there are two things you can never accurately pre-determine: what a jury will decide and who a woman will marry. I was impressed by this during a term of court I held in the Low Country several years ago.

Now, it is established routine for an attorney who brings an action for personal injuries on behalf of his client to ask the trial jury to award actual damages sustained and also punitive damages. The latter are not awarded as compensation for a loss but by way of punishment for a defendant who has been more than negligently wrong. Lawyers are always especially glad to get a verdict for punitive damages in behalf of a client. However, punitive damages cannot be awarded unless actual damages are also allowed.

At the end of the trial, I had sent the jury out with proper instructions relative to actual and punitive damages. The jurors deliberated about one hour and returned to the courtroom undecided.

"Judge, I want to ask you a question," the foreman said.

"Go right ahead," I told him.

"How do you spell punitive?"

I told him how and the jurors returned to their room to continue deliberations.

This development set the plaintiff's lawyer smiling from ear to ear. He figured that he had the rabbit run into the gum for sure and that the jury was all set to close the gum door for him.

His joy was short-lived.

About five minutes later the jury returned declaring, "We find for the defendant."

So, I agreed with my daddy, at least halfway. You can't ever tell what a jury is going to decide.

# APPELLATE WORK

## *Qualified For Robing*

It became the duty of the House of Representatives and the Senate, in joint assembly, to elect a member of the Supreme Court in 1966 because of the death of Chief Justice Claude A. Taylor. I, along with three others, sought the office. There are one hundred seventy members of the General Assembly and a majority vote was necessary for election. The joint assembly voted thirty-six times over a period of thirteen weeks, but no one was able to get a majority.

The election was carried over until the January 1967 meeting. This meant that the solicitation of votes continued for approximately one year. In January 1967, only two remained in contest and I was elected.

Five days after my election I received a form letter from the Secretary of State, which read as follows: "This is to notify you that at a meeting of the joint assembly of the South Carolina Legislature, held on the 15th of January, 1967, you were elected to the office of Associate Justice of the Supreme Court of South Carolina."

It was routine for one of the secretaries in the office of the Secretary of State to notify all persons elected to the boards, trustees, etc. by the legislature.

I wrote my old friend, Secretary of State Frank Thornton, back as follows: "Dear Frank: I have received your letter dated January 30, 1967, and thank you very much for the relevant information which it contained. I must confess that I was aware that a vacancy existed. When you are in the State House next time, would you kindly advise the members of the Senate and of the House that your message has been conveyed to me, and that I have consented to serve. Cordially yours, Bruce Littlejohn."

## *Conditional Compromise*

During the summer of 1966, those of us who sought to be elected Associate Justice of the Supreme Court were contacting all persons who were campaigning for seats in the General Assembly, since the members were to bring about the election. Only 124 House members and 46 Senators were to be elected, but more than 300 candidates were seeking the offices. We made contact with the unopposed candidates first, but it was also necessary to contact all other candidates, since no one knew who was to be elected. Obviously, we were contacting many who would not be in Columbia at the time the vote was to be taken the following January.

About two weeks before the election was to be held, I visited Jack Garrett, who was running for the House of Representatives in Greenville County. I asked him to help me in my bid for the office.

He replied, "You may be wasting your time. I don't know that I am going to be elected. I could just as easily get beat."

I proposed a compromise by saying, "Jack, don't let that worry you. Go ahead and pledge your support to me, and if you are defeated I will promptly release you from your commitment."

## *Justice By The Board*

When the new Spartanburg County Courthouse was completed in 1958, I moved my office as circuit judge into that building.

There was a directory in the main lobby informing people the numbers of rooms where offices were located, including this identification: "Judge Littlejohn, Room 259." Over the years many people came there to see me on business.

When I became a member of the South Carolina Supreme Court in 1967, my name and title remained the same on the directory. Most of my work then was in research, and few people had occasion to be looking for me. At the same time, many people seeing my name on the board continued to come, not realizing the nature of my new work.

One day when I was chatting with Dewey Blanton, the County Administrator, I told him of the fact that many people were coming to my office through error.

"You know, Dewey," I told him, "many people looking for a judge don't know what kind of a judge they are seeking. Many who want to see a circuit judge, the county judge, a magistrate, the probate judge, the judge of the family court, or the master in equity, all of whom are called judge, still come to my office. They are wasting their time, and occasionally it disrupts my secretary, who may be working on something important."

Cooperative and resourceful, Dewey promptly proposed an ingenious solution.

"Bruce, I can put an end to your problem. Actually, your title is no longer 'Judge.' A member of the Supreme Court is more properly called 'Justice.' I will change 'Judge Littlejohn' to Justice Littlejohn. Everybody would like to have a judge, but I don't know of anybody that's looking for justice."

I concluded that Dewey was correct. After the sign was changed, few people came to my office.

## *The Last Shall Be First*

In the Supreme Court, seniority establishes certain procedures. For example, one of the attendants serves water to the members while we are in session in the courtroom. It has been routine for many years that he serves the Chief Justice first; then he serves the senior Associate Justice and so on until the junior Associate Justice is served last.

Not long after I had become the junior Associate Justice, I approached the attendant early one morning before my brothers had arrived at the court. Taking a dollar bill out of my pocket, I showed it to him and rubbed it gently while saying, "I get thirsty before the other members of the court; today I am wondering if you couldn't just serve me first."

The attendant said that he wasn't sure whether he ought to do that or not. It was contrary to his instructions and he indicated that he would have to think about it first. I knew what he was going to actually do in lieu of thinking about it. He was going to ask Miss Frances Smith, the Clerk, for whom he worked, if he could follow the new routine and accept my money.

Next morning the attendant came to me in private and said, "Judge, I can't do that for you. Miss Frances says we got to serve water by seniority."

I put on an appearance of sincerity and said to him, "Why that's ridiculous. I never heard tell of this seniority. Just what is it?"

He explained, "Judge, I don't understood it neither. But whatever it is, Miss Frances say you ain't got none."

### *The Sequel*

A few days later the attendant came to me and said that he had decided to serve me first if I still had the money. I gave him the dollar and drank first that day. Later I learned that the Chief Justice had conspired with him to get my money and told him to serve me first and say nothing about it. Drinking water first on the Supreme Court is great, but drinking water last isn't bad either.

## *Upgrading Possible Potential*

One of the most beloved teachers I ever had was Professor Charles Elliott of the University of South Carolina Law School. He taught Property Law and was an eminent expert whom lawyers all over the state sought to associate in the trial of major cases in which titles to real estate were involved.

When he retired, his friends honored him with a banquet at the Wade Hampton Hotel in Columbia. I was flattered when Senator Marshall Williams of Orangeburg asked me to be master of ceremonies. Circuit Judge James Spruill of Cheraw was present, and I told this basically true story about him:

"I am delighted to see my friend, Judge James Spruill, here tonight. Professor Elliott was one of my instructors and Judge Spruill was also. After I had finished the freshman course at Carolina Law School, Judge Spruill, who had just graduated at the time, agreed to come back and teach Bills and Notes, and so when I was a junior he taught the course to our class.

"Recently, I happened to run into a transcript of my law school record, and I observed that the only 'D' I made while at Law School was given to me by fatherly Professor Spruill, and that's how he graded my papers. However, every dog has his day, and all things come to him who waits. Now that Jim is on the Circuit Court and I am on the Supreme Court, I am going to grade his papers."

Then I turned toward Judge Spruill and said, "Now, Jim, if it develops that instead of affirming or reversing one of your orders, I just put a great big 'D' on it, you will know I just barely let you by."

The story had this sequel: Jim commented, "Now that Bruce is on the Supreme Court and grading my papers, I am mighty glad that I let Professor Ben Hodges talk me into moving his grade up to a 'D'."

### *Scintillating Retort*

In 1970 the Supreme Court moved from the State Capitol Building to new quarters developed in the former Post Office Building. The members of our court were proud of the magnificent new facilities and invited all lawyers and interested citizens to attend an open house. Hundreds of guests came. We formed a receiving line and welcomed all who attended.

After the reception was over, the five justices met briefly in the conference room. All of us were commenting about the fact that the visitors were favorably impressed by the courtroom and building.

In fun, I said to my brothers on the court, "Many of the lawyers commented that with such a fine building as this, hereafter they would expect the rest of you on the court to write legal opinions as good as mine."

My colleague Justice Woodrow Lewis, well-known for his dry wit, was equal to the situation.

He retorted, "Well, that certainly is not too high a standard for the people to expect."

## *Stamp Of Disapproval*

Until about 1970, the South Carolina Supreme Court held its sessions in the State House in Columbia. Many years ago the space provided there was sufficient, but as the court's work load increased it became necessary for it to have more room, so the Legislature bought the old post office building at the corner of Sumter and Gervais streets. Most post offices don't resemble a courthouse, but this one did. When the architects and contractor reworked the interior, it ended up a rather magnificent facility which the justices have enjoyed.

A lawyer who lost a case before us was a former patron of the old post office and had bought stamps and mailed letters there during his academic and law school student days.

After losing, he was overheard to mutter, "I believe they administered more justice there when they sold stamps."

## *On The House?*

One of the first cases to come before the Supreme Court after I became a member was one requiring a ruling on the validity of an order by a judge of the Richland County Court.

That order had effectually enjoined the law enforcement officers from enforcing the state liquor law and permitted the Pirate Cove Lounge in Columbia to operate a bar. Our court held that this was illegal and reversed the lower court.

Shortly thereafter I was in Charleston and went to lunch at a local restaurant with Federal District Court Judge Charles Simons and State Circuit Judge James Spruill, who were presiding over sessions of court in that city. After we had placed our order, the waiter suggested that we might enjoy a cocktail or a highball while our food was being prepared.

Judge Simons inquired, "Say, fellow, did you know that this is Justice Littlejohn of the Supreme Court, which held a few days ago that serving whiskey in a restaurant is illegal in this state?"

The waiter apologized, looked frightened, excused himself, and backed through the door, keeping his eye on all of us as he departed. Several minutes later he returned, smiling, and said, "Gentlemen, the manager say what I really meant was he wanted to give you all a drink 'cause they don't sell nothing here."

## *Fixings For Five*

Judge William H. Grimball Sr. was resident circuit judge of the Charleston and Berkeley counties circuit. He served for many years and was one of South Carolina's most distinguished jurists.

Once, while presiding over Cherokee County Common Pleas Court in Gaffney, he completed an exhaustive charge to the jury in a personal injury case. Within fifteen or twenty minutes he covered a lot of ground. He explained to the jury the meaning of the pleadings, the judge's part in the trial, and the duty of the jury. He defined willfulness and wantonness and detailed the laws covering contributory negligence, accident and imminent peril. Further, he described actual and punitive damages and unavoidable accident.

When he finished, having pumped the well dry as far as applicable legalities were concerned, and the jury had retired to deliberate, a lawyer approached him and observed, "Judge, you know those twelve old men on the jury didn't understand all that you were explaining to them."

Judge Grimball, wise in the ways of courts and knowing that if he didn't "tell it like it is" in his charge, one side or the other would appeal to the State Supreme Court, sagely confided to his lawyer friend, "I wasn't particularly talking to those twelve old men. I was mostly talking to those five old men on the Supreme Court in Columbia."

## *"Chief" Grounded*

In 1967 the American Bar Association and the Judges Conference met in Honolulu.

Among those attending from South Carolina were Chief Justice Joseph R. Moss of York, Associate Justice Thomas Bussey of Charleston and myself of the Supreme Court, and Circuit Judges George Gregory of Chester and William L. Rhodes Jr. of Hampton.

Justice Moss and I flew together to Honolulu but were booked on separate planes for the trip back to Los Angeles. My plane arrived in Los Angeles on time, enabling me to get the next flight to Atlanta. Chief Justice Moss' plane was due to arrive in L. A. at nearly the same time but was running late. I waited until takeoff time before boarding the Atlanta plane and then asked an attendant if he would hold it for a few minutes because I was expecting "my boss" to arrive momentarily.

"What kind of work does your boss do?" he asked.

Facetiously, I said, "He doesn't do any kind of work—he's the chief."

That did it. "We can't wait," the attendant decreed. "We've got too many Indians on this plane already."

With that he pulled up the "gangplank," and Justice Moss was left behind in Los Angeles.

## *Poetic Decision*

During an Appellate Judicial Conference in Dallas I attended a session where Dr. Cooley of Houston and Professor Freund of Harvard were on a panel.

Dr. Cooley, a noted surgeon, had performed about thirty-nine heart transplants at that time. He and Professor Freund, who was well-known in academic and legal circles for his outstanding ability, were discussing the Uniform Organ Transplant Law. Listening, I learned that doctors are very much afraid that they may remove a vital organ from the body of a supposedly dead person before total expiration and be sued. Because of this hazard, doctors and surgeons all over the United States want this law. Among the questions they sought to have resolved by the law was a definition of "When is a man dead?" Previously I had thought that all doctors were able to agree on this point. But I learned during the discussion that they differ. Some think a person dies when the brain stops functioning; others believe that death occurs when the heart ceases to beat; and some contend that life ends when the victim's nervous reactions disappear.

Being unable to agree, they wrote the Uniform Organ Transplant Law and omitted the definition. One day, perhaps, some judge, with legal help,may undertake to define, "When is a man dead?"

Since that time, I read a newspaper account about the family of a man whose heart had been transplanted; they were suing the transplanting doctors, contending his heart had been removed before death actually occurred. Thus, this fear among doctors appears to be well founded.

An ingenious lawyer friend of mine also listened to the panel and while the discussion was underway, he scribbled this definition of his own:

He is not dead,
Who from the bed,
Can still arise and sue.
But he is dead beyond debate,
Who from the bed
Can't litigate.

## *Bargain Basemented*

When I attended the Appellate Judges Conference in Dallas about 1969, Chief Justice Joseph R. Moss and I walked down the street from our hotel to the Neiman-Marcus Store. We found everything just as elaborate and expensive as it had been described. One may find a necktie for nineteen dollars or thirty-nine dollars or fifty-nine dollars—and other things correspondingly expensive.

We drifted over to the jewelry department and observed a number of ladies' pins under a glass counter. I pointed one out to the clerk and asked him if I might see it. He obliged by removing it from the counter, placing it on a black velvet tray and, while holding the tray with both hands, sort of presented it to me. It was very pretty and I asked the price, to which he responded "four hundred dollars."

Chief Justice Moss smiled as though to suggest, "Why don't you get a dozen?" Not to be outdone, I said to the clerk, "I had in mind something a little more exquisite, even if it costs more money. Do you have anything better?"

He responded, "Why certainly." And then he looked around and found another, placed it on a black velvet tray and presented it.

I said to him, "Now this one is obviously better. How much does it cost?"

To this he replied, "This one is five thousand, five hundred dollars."

I told him, "You know, I drive an Oldsmobile ninety-eight —that's the biggest one they make. It has air conditioning, power windows, power seats, a.m. and f.m. radio, and all the trimmings. The whole thing only cost five thousand, three hundred dollars."

To this the clerk replied, "Well, if you drive an Oldsmobile, perhaps you would like to shop in our bargain basement."

# OTHER COURTS AND JUDGES

## *Ego Evaporated*

Federal Judge Cecil Wyche was one of Spartanburg's outstanding attorneys. For many years he was a leading trial lawyer, a learned student of the law and a skilled politician. He practiced law with James F. Byrnes from 1924 to 1930. Along about 1936, Byrnes, then in the U. S. Senate, backed Wyche for appointment by President Roosevelt as U. S. District Judge.

Wyche took great pride in his office and proceeded on the theory that everybody ought to know that he was the Federal judge. Some of his friends used to chide him a little and say that he was one of the few people who could strut while sitting down.

But one night at a banquet in Spartanburg I saw his ego somewhat deflated. We were attending a banquet together, preceded by a cocktail party at seven with the banquet beginning at eight. About five minutes to eight the lights were dimmed, signaling that the bar was about to be closed, so we went to the dining area to be served. Seated with Judge Wyche and me was John C. Williams Sr., who at that time was U. S. District Attorney.

The food service was slow, so Judge Wyche, in his typical gruff voice, called to a waiter and said, "Boy co'mere. If you're not going to give me any food, go back there and get me another drink." The waiter left but quickly returned to report, "Judge, the bar has been closed. They wouldn't give me a drink for you."

Mr. Williams immediately volunteered, "Judge, you just sit right there. I'll get you a drink. Don't you worry. I'll find you a drink somewhere."

About five minutes later he returned with a drink, handed it to the judge and said, "Judge, it wasn't easy. I told them I had to have a drink for you, and you know what the bartender said?" Judge Wyche curiously queried expecting a compliment, "What did he say about me?"

Mr. Williams quoted: "He says, 'You know, I believe I knows that Judge Wyche. Say, ain't he the magistrate up at Campobello?"

## *Not For Fifty Dollars!*

Before Cecil Wyche became a U. S. District Judge, he had a large and varied legal practice. He represented clients on both sides of the court and developed a reputation in defending persons charged with crime. His experiences were numerous and sometimes colorful, in and out of court, including this one:

One Sunday morning a man telephoned him at his home, insisting that he had to see him immediately. Wyche told him he did not go to his law office on Sunday and asked the man to meet him there Monday, but the caller persisted, so it was finally agreed that they would confer on the Sabbath Day.

Upon arriving at his office, the lawyer found impatiently awaiting him a highly agitated man who said another man was fiddling around with his wife.

"I'm gonna kill him, I can't let him live another day," the man declared. "I know they are gonna put me in jail, and I know I got to stand trial, and I want to employ you right now to take care of my interests."

Choosing, lawyer-like, to put first things first, Wyche asked him, "How much money do you have?"

To this, the man responded, "I've got fifty dollars."

Wyche described the end of the conference: "I told him, 'Don't kill him.' "

## *Accelerated Eloquency*

During World War II quite a few people were charged with black marketing. A defendant residing in Union was brought to Spartanburg to plead guilty in Federal Court to a charge of violating the rationing law. He was represented by P. D.

Barron, a noted trial attorney. I have heard several attorneys declare that Barron was perhaps the best all-round trial attorney they had ever known.

When the guilty plea was entered, Mr. Barron began bragging on his client before Judge Cecil Wyche. He related that he had lived honestly and honorably all his life, had never been in court before, had bought war bonds and worked with the Red Cross. Finally, he argued that probation was the best solution in this case.

Judge Wyche had on his desk a probation officer's pre-trial investigation report. Referring to this, he disclosed, "Mr. Barron, apparently you are not aware of the fact that this defendant told the probation officer he did not want to go on probation under any circumstances."

Normally this would have floored the average attorney, but not Mr. Barron. Immediately, in his eloquent manner, he explained, "Your Honor, my client is not a learned man. He didn't have the advantage of much schooling. He understandeth not the English language as you and I. I am certain that the thought my client intended to convey to the probation officer and this court was that hereafter he is going to behave himself in such an honorable fashion that it won't be necessary to even put him on probation."

Judge Wyche smiled and observed, "Mr. Barron, I have never seen you at a loss for words. Today is no exception."

## *Handle With Care*

Judge Wyche was one of those judges who liked to inject their personal participation in the trial of a case. Some judges say almost nothing during a trial except to rule on motions or objections. They let the lawyers run the show. There are others who get right into the middle of the fight by asking questions or making suggestions to counsel, hopefully maneuvering toward a proper termination and a just verdict.

Judge Wyche, sometimes enthusiastically, was one of the latter, as in a case in Columbia when a young lawyer was conducting his first trial before the Spartanburg jurist. Somewhere along the line the judge more or less took over the case and began asking questions and otherwise participating, but on the side of the young attorney.

Finally the exasperated lawyer admonished the court, "Now Judge, I have prepared this case well and I think I can win it. If you're gonna take charge, just be sure you don't lose it."

## *Travel Troubles*

Both state and federal courts from about 1935 to 1955 handled many cases involving illegal manufacture, possession and sale of whisky. We uplanders called it "gully liquor"; others called it "white lightning", and in lower South Carolina it was called "stump hole liquor."

Many defendants charged with making or selling this brand of fire water were too old to work or were crippled or partly disabled. Of course, healthy people were also engaged in the illegal liquor business. It was an easy way to make money.

Judge Wyche once had before him an elderly man who pleaded guilty to selling illegal whisky. At sentencing time, the judge told the defendant, "I don't know what to do with you. You've been up before; you've been sentenced before. Obviously, you are not in the best of health."

Then, exploring the possibilities, none of which opened the freedom door to the defendant, the judge said, "I could send you to a federal prison in Texas, or I could send you to one down in Florida; they have a federal prison out in Kansas and another in Virginia where I could send you."

The defendant thereby was noticed that he would have to serve some time, but he didn't care for the various distances the various prisons offered.

"Just to tell you the truth, Judge," he implored, "I ain't in no shape to travel."

## *Cooperative*

A defendant in poor health and of minimum mentality, but still shrewd, stood before Judge Wyche for sentencing after entering his latest guilty plea on a bootlegging charge.

"You're a problem to me," Judge Wyche said. "I just don't know what to do with you. It worries me."

The defendant was both sympathetic and clever.

"If it will be of any help to you," he suggested, "let's both forget about the whole thing."

## *Bargain Moonshine*

Judge Thomas S. Sease became Resident Judge of the Seventh Judicial Circuit in 1909. About twenty-five years later his nephew Cecil Wyche was appointed United States District Court Judge, with offices in Spartanburg just across the street from the County Court House, where Judge Sease held much court.

About that time, which was in the middle 1930s, both the Federal and the State Courts processed many cases where men were charged with making corn liquor illegally. It was well-known that Judge Sease liked to take a little drink.

Not long after Judge Wyche was appointed, he was holding his first criminal court in Spartanburg. Judge Sease walked across the street to the Federal Court House to pay his respects to his newly-made judge nephew.

During a recess in chambers, Judge Wyche said, "Uncle Tom, for the first time I am having to pass sentences on defendants charged with making liquor. How much do you give these bootleggers?"

Without batting an eye, Judge Sease retorted, "Never more than two dollars a gallon."

## *Deserted In Crisis*

One of the most delightful fellows I worked with as a circuit judge was George Collins, a court reporter who for some twenty years efficiently served the circuit courts in Columbia. George had an accumulation of stories and was gifted in relating them. One of his favorites involved Circuit Judge Thomas S. Sease and a certain court incident in Columbia.

A defendant without a lawyer was being questioned by the solicitor who asked a question which was not material.

"Don't answer that question," His Honor protectively told the defendant and then warned, "Mr. Solicitor, this man has no lawyer. Stay within the rules."

The over-diligent solicitor put another question, also not material.

Judge Sease again cautioned the witness to keep silent and once more warned the solicitor.

The solicitor made a third try but didn't score.

"Mr. Solicitor," the veteran jurist repeated, "that question is irrelevant. Don't answer it, Mr. Witness. Stay within the rules, Mr. Solicitor."

Finally, the solicitor threw one right over the plate. His question was one that would have placed the defendant right under the jail, had he answered, so, still trusting his "lawyer on the bench," the defendant hesitated, turned to judge Sease and inquired, "What we say about that, Cap?"

Judge Sease stormed out in his inimitable and familiar thunder, "Go on and answer the question."

The deserted defendant did, the jury retired and wrote a verdict promptly.

He was convicted.

## *Booze Better Than Law*

Judge Thomas S. Sease of the Seventh Circuit had a summer home at Saluda, North Carolina.

After completing his home circuit June and July courts each year he would board the Southern Railway's Carolina Special for the trip from Spartanburg, where he resided, to his summer place up in the Polk County mountains. Before leaving, he heard equity matters during the July term. One summer he asked attorneys on both sides of an equity proceeding to prepare briefs and submit them to him before his departure so he could decide the case while on vacation.

One of the lawyers knew that Judge Sease enjoyed top quality corn liquor, so he delivered his brief and a quart of corn squeezings to the judge at trainside.

Judge Sease habitually asked the prevailing lawyer in such cases to draw a proposed order for his signature. After he had relaxed in the mountains about ten days, he wrote and mailed a note to the lawyer who had given him the liquor.

The missive said, "Your liquor was good but your law was bad. I'm asking the lawyer on the other side to draw up the order."

## *Let's Go To Press*

Greenville County Clerk of Court T. E. Christenberry was one of the most delightful fellows I came to know while traveling the circuits and trying cases. He was a veteran of many years service and enjoyed telling a story on himself. It went like this:

"When I became Clerk of Court no one was greener on the job than I. I goofed on the first day while Judge Thomas S. Sease of Spartanburg was presiding. A jury had returned from its deliberations.

"Judge Sease inquired, 'Gentlemen, have you reached a verdict?'

"The foreman responded, 'We have.'

"The judge turned to me and said, 'Mr. Clerk, would you publish the verdict?'

"I was most anxious to please, and so I replied to His Honor, 'Yes sir, Judge, I will be glad to. Which paper do you want me to have them put it in?' "

## *Baby "Springs" Mom*

Walter Wilkinson, a very able court reporter in the Twelfth Judicial Circuit, served from about 1925 to well up into the 60s. He enjoyed telling this story about a happening in Horry County at Conway, the county seat.

He said that Judge C. J. Ramage of Edgefield was holding criminal court. A lady was charged with assault and battery with intent to kill. In such a case a jury may find a person guilty of assault and battery with intent to kill, or assault and battery of a high and aggravated nature, or of simple assault and battery. The circumstances under which the assault occurred were rather aggravated, but the jury had compassion on the lady because among other things she had a small baby. They gave her substantial benefit of the doubt and found her guilty of simple assault and battery, which carried a penalty of not more than thirty days or a $100 fine. The facts were so aggravated that the judge, without inquiring into the matter at length, just sentenced the lady to thirty days in jail. One of the deputies carried her away from the courtroom.

Walter said that he and the sheriff and the judge were going to lunch together that day. Just as they were leaving the courthouse, two women approached the judge. One of them, a lady about thirty-five years of age, had a small baby riding on her hip, saddle-fashion.

She approached the judge and said, "Say, Mister. I got to have a word with you. That's my sister what you just sent down to jail, and this is her baby, and this woman standing here is her ma. Now we got a sister at home what ain't here today. But Judge," she continued, "this baby needs milk, and me, I ain't got no milk. Her ma here, she ain't got no milk either. Our sister at home ain't got any milk either. And we don't know what the devil we gonna do."

Walter says there was a long moment of silence as the woman with the baby on her hip stared straight into the eyes of the judge.

Finally, Judge Ramage broke the silence by saying, "Lady, don't look at me like that. I ain't got no milk either." And then after another long pause, the judge turned to the sheriff and said, "Sheriff, go down there and turn that woman loose. This baby has got to have some milk."

## *Trail Of Cores*

Circuit judges sometimes become known for having certain characteristics. One stands out because he wears a red necktie all the time. Another may be widely discussed because he passes substantial sentences in criminal cases. Still others may be characterized by their liberal views in civil proceedings, and so on.

Circuit Judge C. J. Ramage, who retired in the late 1930s and was succeeded by Judge Strom Thurmond, was noted because of his fondness for apples. He ate many of them every day. Some of my friends who knew him better than I said he kept a bag-full at the courthouse, another sack-full in his room and more in his automobile all the time, and that he ate one or two during court recesses and usually consumed more at the end of the day.

Once Judge Ramage rotated into the Seventh Judicial Circuit to hold court in Union where he also had jurisdiction over proceedings in Spartanburg, a part of the circuit. A Spartanburg attorney drove to Union to get the judge to sign an order. Arriving about eleven a. m., he didn't find the jurist in the courtroom, so he inquired of the clerk concerning his whereabouts, and was informed:

"You're too late. The judge settled the case assigned for today and has left town. By now, he's probably two apples down the road."

## *Formality Faded*

State Supreme Court Chief Justice Joseph R. Moss enjoys relating this incident, which occurred when he was a circuit judge and holding court in Marion.

He had just been elected to the circuit court and admits that he took great pride in wearing his robe and attempting to preside with utmost dignity and formality. But in Marion he was "taken down" by an elderly lady who apparently had a mind of her own, which definitely excluded the presiding judge and regard for his dignity and high position.

An attorney was cross-examining her diligently but with poor results. She dodged the issue, refused to answer questions and sometimes just sat stubbornly silent in the witness chair.

"Finally, in desperation," Judge Moss relates, "I turned to her and sternly ordered, 'Lady, go ahead and answer the question.'

"Apparently, she discovered me for the first time and retorted, 'What you got to do with it, bub?' "

## *Judicial Ability Helps*

When Chief Justice Moss was a circuit judge and holding court in Columbia, he joined Otis Bruce and Jim Wolfe of Inman, his friends of many years, at a hotel one day for lunch.

When the judge met them he was weary from the morning's proceedings, during which he had found the lawyers on both sides somewhat incompetent and with their cases poorly prepared. In relating this experience, he told them what a delight it was to be in court with good lawyers, and pointed out that "It adds to the joy of a trial if the lawyers involved know the law and how to conduct a trial."

Otis, in his typical dry wit, agreed with the jurist and observed, "They tell me it helps a little bit if the judge knows some law."

## *Jumbled Judges*

Judges Ben Greneker of Edgefield and Badger Baker of Florence were among the judges with whom I rode the circuits for many years.

Our rotating system provided the special pleasure of returning to counties where I had previously presided and also of renewing friendships. It also presented the problem of unsuccessfully trying to remember the names of people I had met earlier. These people remembered judges well because of the fact that not many of us rotated into their areas. Occasionally they mixed-up identities of the judges, as once when I returned to Bishopville to open court, visited the clerk's office where a young lady employee greeted me, "Oh, Judge Greneker, we're certainly glad to have you back in Bishopville again."

Deciding to indulge in light levity, I told her, "Young Lady, you're mistaken. I'm not Judge Greneker. I'm Judge Baker from Florence."

She apologized and hastened to explain, "Oh, Judge Baker, do forgive me. I knew it was you all the time, but I was recording a paper yesterday that Judge Greneker had signed, and I guess I just had him on my mind."

Having "jumbled" judges enough for her, I didn't attempt to straighten her out concerning judicial identities.

## *He Finally Made It*

Judge Ben Greneker enjoyed relating this experience he had in his home town of Edgefield soon after his election to the circuit bench.

In accordance with custom, he was holding summer courts in his home circuit, where for several years he previously had periodically represented a bootlegger when he had stood trial or pleaded guilty. The legal fee had always been $100.

Early Monday morning around breakfast time, and with court due to open within a few hours, the judge's bootlegger friend called at his home, informed that he was again charged with violating the liquor law and needed an attorney forthwith. Judge Greneker told him, "I am now the judge, and it will not be possible for me to serve as your lawyer any more. When you get to court you will find me sitting on the bench instead of trying cases."

His friend listened patiently until the judge had finished and then exclaimed, "Aw, Mr. Greneker, let's don't be technical. Go ahead and take this hundred dollars like you used to and do the best you can for me."

* * *

Ben Greneker practiced law some twenty-five years in Edgefield and other counties and retired as circuit judge after serving approximately twenty years in that office. Under the state's retirement system, a judge is permitted to practice law after he retires but may not make courtroom appearances. Within a few days after he opened his law office in Edgefield upon retirement, one of his friends, an elderly lady from the country, came by his office and saw his shingle hanging out. She didn't understand about his long career but greeted him, "Mr. Greneker, I shore am glad they finally admitted you to practice law."

## *Holdout Exposed*

All events transpiring in a jury room are supposed to be secret. They usually are.

Normally, it is considered improper for a juror to disclose how the various members of his panel stood in regard to a case while it was being deliberated, but occasionally slip-ups occur, as in Manning where Circuit Judge T. B. Greneker was holding court.

A jury received a case, left the courtroom and stayed out for a long time. Finally, the judge called the jurors back and told them he hoped they would endeavor to agree on a verdict. He then asked the foreman, "Do you think you are going to be able to agree?"

Pointing his finger, the foreman promptly divulged, "Judge, we've agreed already, all 'cept Mr. Smith what's sitting on the end of the row down there."

## *Streaking Futile*

Spartanburg County Family Court Judge Paul S. McChesney does an extraordinarily fine job of handling cases which involve feuds between husbands and wives, adoptions and domestic relations cases in general. He has had many varied experiences and enjoys relating this occurrence.

A husband brought a divorce action against his wife on the ground of adultery. During the trial the husband, as plaintiff, related:

"I came home sort of unexpected one day and walked into the house. My wife was there. I didn't see any other man, but there was a strange pair of pants laying on the floor. I turned to her and asked, 'Where is the s. o. b.?' I didn't get a very satisfactory answer, so I went to a dresser drawer and got out my forty-five. I loaded it with bullets and looked under the bed. He wasn't there. I looked in the closets on the first floor and he wasn't there. I looked in all the adjoining rooms but I couldn't find him. So I went downstairs into the basement and I looked in all of the rooms down there, and he couldn't be found.

"Finally, I remembered that there was a closet at the end of the hall in the basement. So, I walked down there and opened the door. I couldn't see anybody until I pushed the clothes hanging on the rod back to the side.

"There he was, standing in the closet behind the hanging clothes, and all he had on was a T-shirt.

"I demanded, 'What in the hell are you doing here?' and he replied, 'Everybody has got to be somewhere.' "

## *Probate Judge J. William Davenport*

Probate Judge J. William Davenport of Spartanburg has a lot of unusual experiences, the same as a trial judge. His duties require him to administer the estates of deceased persons and issue marriage licenses. He also performs a great many marriage ceremonies. Thousands of ceremonies are routine but—like man bites dog—one made considerable news.

Bill has an unusual capacity to spot a phony, but one slipped by and he enjoys telling this one on himself:

"What appeared to be a normal couple came to my office from Charlotte. I was misled to believe that one of them was a man and the other a woman. The deceit was not brought about by the conventional girl wearing blue jeans and the young man who oftentimes wears his hair down to the shoulders. This pair were well-dressed and groomed—one like a man and the other like a woman.

"Some time after I had performed a marriage ceremony joining the two in wedlock, I learned that both of them were women. The woman posing as a counterfeit man had worked along with her partner for several years. Later the true facts were revealed and the story got much publicity in this country and abroad."

"One of my friends has asked me what precautions I now take to prevent such a thing happening again. I told him that I make a cursory examination to be sure there is no error. My friend asked me how I go about making a cursory examination to tell whether the applicant for a license is a man or a woman. I told him that I thump them, like a farmer thumps a watermelon to detect whether it is ripe or not. If it sounds plink, I know it's a girl. If it sounds plunk, I know it's a boy."

* * *

Judge Davenport also enjoys telling about a widow who came to his office to apply for letters of administration on her deceased husband's estate. She brought with her one of her neighbors. While they were filling out some papers incident to application for administration, the neighbor commented, "I don't know a thing in the world about probate matters."

To this the widow responded, "I can well understand. I would be just as ignorant as you are if my husband hadn't been a notary public."

## *Smithsonian Psychology*

Mrs. Ellen Hines Smith, Chief Judge of the Spartanburg Civil and Criminal Court, grinds out a mass of business and does an excellent job of disposing of small claims. In addition to having knowledge of the law, she has a good understanding of people and from time to time pours oil on troubled waters by using psychology and common sense.

Judge Smith enjoys reciting this incident which happened in her court:

"I tried a small claims matter in which a seventy-year-old carpenter was suing his seventy-three-year-old friend for sixty dollars, alleging that he was entitled to be paid for repairing his friend's porch. As plaintiff, the carpenter alleged that he was entitled to three dollars per hour for his labor, but his defendant-friend contended that he was too old to collect the same amount he might have collected in his youth, arguing that age had made him a jackleg carpenter worth less than three dollars per hour.

"After hearing all the evidence, I gave judgment for the plaintiff-carpenter in the amount of sixty dollars, indicating that it represented thirty hours of work at two dollars per hour.

"The plaintiff-carpenter jumped to his feet shouting, 'There's no justice in the world! You can't rob a man of honest wages.' "

Judge Smith says that she quickly concluded that there must be some way to help this outraged litigant save his face and protect his pride. She came through with an amended judgment which solved the problem when she said, "I have reconsidered the matter. I withdraw the judgment and instead I find for the plaintiff the sum of sixty dollars, which represents twenty hours work at three dollars per hour."

"The plaintiff-carpenter smiled, shook my hand gratefully and left, convinced that the amended verdict did justice in the case."

## *Once Over Lightly*

The rotation system for circuit judges in South Carolina requires them to travel the entire state in holding courts. Eventually, judges will double back to counties where they have previously presided.

Twelfth Judicial Circuit Judge L. D. Lide of Marion enjoyed relating this incident which occurred when he doubled back for court in Georgetown.

He said he arose early one morning and headed for a barber shop for a shave. The barber lathered him well and began rapidly whipping his straight razor up and down a razor strop to give it a keen edge.

Just before he began mowing the judge's whiskers, he asked, "Judge Lide, do you remember me?"

"No, I don't believe I do," His Honor replied.

The barber enlightened him. "When you were holding court here several years ago, you sentenced me to two years."

The Judge eyed him and said, "Once over lightly will be sufficient. Skip the neck. I don't need a close shave today."

## *Brevity Pays Off*

I cannot recall having ever heard a speech that was too short, but I've heard many that were too long. Circuit Judge G. Duncan Bellinger related this incident, in point:

A husband charged with assault and battery upon another man was tried before him in Lexington. The State contended that the defendant came home around midnight, found a surplus man there with his wife and shot him.

The defendant did not have an attorney, so Judge Bellinger guided him in procedure, this being before the time when practically all indigent defendants were supplied court-appointed counsel. When the time came to argue the case before the jury, the judge told the defendant he could address the panel and make a speech. He accepted the invitation.

Standing before the jury, he discarded any effort at eloquence and simply said, "Gentlemen, I ain't done what they claim I done and I don't know how to make a speech. But if when you get home tonight, you find at your house what they said was at my house and you don't do what they said I did, you ain't much of a man." Then he stopped and returned to his seat.

Judge Bellinger charged the jurors and they left the courtroom to deliberate. Five minutes later they came back.

"Not guilty," the foreman reported.

## *My Time Is Your Time*

Usually when a defendant is about to be sentenced in court, he becomes very repentant, or at least pretends to be. Lawyers and some others around courthouses have a saying that a man will admit and say just about anything when "his belly is against the rail."

Down in Charleston Circuit Judge Steve Griffith of Newberry was holding criminal court when a man about twenty years of age pleaded guilty to armed robbery. He was of the "tough as nails" type. As is customary, the judge asked the defendant, "Is there anything you have to say before I pronounce sentence?" Just as he completed the question, the chimes at a nearby church rang five times for five o'clock in the afternoon. When the chimes ceased, the judge repeated his question.

The defendant gazed bitterly at the judge, looked at a clock on the wall, looked back at the judge and grimly informed him, "Your clock is five minutes fast."

## *Carpool Delayed*

Judge G. B. Greene of Anderson was a veteran jurist of the earlier years, when South Carolina had fourteen judicial circuits and each judge traveled two of them, plus his home area, each year. Under this rotation system it took seven years for a judge to complete his state-wide swing and return to the same county again.

This system once placed one of Judge Greene's defendants on the long end of a circuitous trip. This occurred on a Friday when he was about to close a term in Newberry and was preparing to sentence the last defendant before heading back to Anderson.

Responding to the judge's inquiry if he had anything to say in his own behalf, the culprit related several flattering things about himself and then remarked, "Judge, you know I come originally from Anderson, the same as you."

This nudge for sympathy alerted the judge, who queried the defendant, "Let me ask you something. Let's suppose just for a moment that I was the defendant and you were the judge, what kind of sentence would you pass and what would you do?"

The defendant, apparently thinking the door to leniency had been opened or at least widely cracked, responded, "Judge, I would say, 'Come on, let's you and me go back to Anderson together.' And I would give you a free ride."

Judge Greene smiled and replied, "Well, you may have a good idea. I hold court in Newberry every seven years, and what I am going to do is pick you up on the next trip around. The sentence of the court is that you be confined at hard labor for seven years."

## *Witnesses Give The Strangest Answers*

When Judge Dan Laney of Bishopville was trying criminal cases in Spartanburg, Solicitor John H. Nolen had a witness on the stand and was endeavoring to have him identify the defendant. Of the witness Solicitor Nolen inquired, "Do you see the defendant in the courtroom today?"

The witness replied, "Yes, sir."

"Would you point him out?"

"He is sitting at the table with defense counsel."

Solicitor Nolen pried further, "Which one is he?"

"He's second from the left end and third from the right end." The witness responded.

"What kind of a coat does he have on?"

"A green striped coat."

The defendant was sitting at the table with his chin in his right hand, sort of propped up. The solicitor, wanting to still further identify the defendant, inquired, "Mr. Witness, where is his right hand?"

The witness was just as serious in his answer as the solicitor had been with his question when he replied, "It's on the end of his arm."

* * *

Judge Ellen Hines Smith tells about a wife who came to her office one day to apply for a warrant against her husband, whom she was accusing of assault and battery.

In order to understand the problem a little more fully, the Judge inquired of her, "Where did he hit you?"

The wife replied, "In the kitchen."

* * *

Probate Judge William Davenport tells about a widow who came to his office for the purpose of applying for letters of administration upon the estate of her late husband, who had just died. They proceeded to fill out the forms until they got to the blank on the form which requires a listing of his personal and real property.

The Judge inquired, "What did he have?"

The lady replied, "Pneumonia."

## *The Court Was Candid*

Bill McGowan was an attorney in Greenwood, where he also doubled as city court recorder. Like most other recorders ( city judges ), he dealt with a number of interesting cases. One involved an assault and battery case against a man who was charged with beating his wife—somewhat, but not severely.

After she had testified, the defendant testified and contended that his wife was a constant nagger. He related her constant complaining and other cantankerous conduct in and about the house.

Then he queried Recorder McGowan, "Judge, let me ask you, suppose your wife nagged at you like my wife nags at me, what would you do?"

The court was candid.

"I would run like a cat being chased by a dog," the recorder replied.

## *Food For Thought*

Most jurors enjoy eating, especially at county expense. Their appetites sometimes can affect their deliberations and delay the returning of their verdicts.

On one occasion, a jury was deliberating and time passed slowly. The judge and clerk of court were attempting to decide whether to send them out for lunch or keep them in session awhile longer, hoping they'd bring in a verdict so court could be recessed and everybody could go home.

Finally, the clerk suggested, "Judge, let me step over to the door. Maybe I can hear something that will give us a clue whether they are going to agree on a verdict or not."

He placed one ear near the door, listened, smiled and returned to the judge.

"What did you hear?" the judge asked.

"All I heard, the clerk informed him, "was one of 'em said, 'I ain't gonna agree to nothing until that s. o. b. in the black robe feeds us some lunch!"

They ate.

## *Never Look Back*

During the trial of an action back in the 1960s, with a guest passenger suing a vehicle driver, the evidence showed that at the time of the incident involved, two Wofford College students were out double dating. Testimony by various witnesses pieced these circumstances together:

As they were driving back, the girl on the rear seat of the car revealed for the first time that she was married, but said she and her husband were separated and would be divorced soon. Also, she said her husband didn't object to her dating.

About that time they arrived at her home to drop her off; her angry husband loomed up in the glare of the headlights and reached down for a brick. The driver, fearing trouble, threw his car into low gear and took off at high speed. Too quickly—miles away, he ran across a railroad track, lost control of the car and wrecked.

They were not aware that the husband had dropped the brick and decided not to pursue.

In the trial, the question arose as to whether the driver was justified in his rapid flight. On cross-examination, an attorney asked him why he fled so fast and so far and queried, "Couldn't you have looked back and detected that you were not being pursued?"

The driver smiled and aptly quipped, "A rabbit never looks back to see where the dogs are."

## *Do-It-Yourself Kit*

Court recorders in Spartanburg and other municipalities have a tough time in their dealings with chronic drunks.

Spartanburg once had a more or less "regular," whom we will call Backus. Habitually, he was back in court not more than two days after his latest release and after another bout with the bottle. I was told that he stayed in the city jail so frequently and so long that he gave his permanent address as 145 Broad Street, the location of the bastille and city hall. Further, I was informed that during one calendar year he was incarcerated there for more than eleven months on about twenty to twenty-five fifteen-day or fifteen dollars fine sentences.

One Monday morning when he came up for sentencing again, the recorder greeted him, "Backus, you have been here so often, you have heard me pass many sentences, and you have been sentenced by me so often that you know how to sentence people as well as I do. And so today, instead of the judge sentencing you, I am going to let you sentence yourself."

Backus responded to the proposition with dignity.

"Backus, stand up," he ordered himself.

Then he solemnly intoned, "Backus, the sentence of the court is that you be confined to the city jail for a period of fifteen days, but the sentence is suspended." Next he retrieved his hat, clamped it on his head and departed the courtroom.

But Backus, being a man of unceasing thirst, was weak. His self-granted leniency didn't work.

The judge waited two days, then Backus was back in court. This time the judge passed his own sentence.

# POLITICAL POTPOURRI

## *A Cherished Blessing*

When I first started to run for circuit judge I was about thirty-six and my father was around seventy-five. He was one of the first persons to know my plans to leave politics and the practice of law to seek a judgeship.

It is not easy for parents to realize that their children have grown up, and I suspect that this especially applies to the "baby of the family," I being the youngest of their eight. When I told my father I wanted to run for the judgeship, hoping to succeed the late Thomas S. Sease, long-resident judge of the Seventh South Carolina Judicial Circuit, he asked candidly, "Son, do you think you have sense enough to be a judge?"

Equally candid, I replied, "Pop, frankly, I do not have sense enough to be a judge. I'm not at all sure that anybody's got sense enough to be a judge, but I want to assure you of this: I've got just as much sense as those other candidates who also want to be a judge."

Smiling, he affectionately gave me his blessing: "Son, I hope you beat 'em."

## *Judicial "Grand Juror"*

About 1951, the South Carolina Veterans of Foreign Wars held their state convention in Spartanburg. One of the events incident thereto was a cocktail party and banquet celebration at the old Officers' Clubhouse at Camp Croft, then headquarters for the Spartanburg VFW Club.

The party had been set up for seven o'clock with the banquet to begin at eight. The main speaker of the evening was Governor James F. Byrnes. Among those present was my friend

Justice Claude Taylor of the South Carolina Supreme Court, who later became Chief Justice.

Mrs. Littlejohn and I arrived at the clubhouse about a quarter till eight. As we entered, an old friend was leaving. I call him an old friend, even though I did not know his name at the time and cannot call it now. I recognized his face and knew he was among those who had helped me in my legislative campaigns in Spartanburg County. It was obvious that he had arrived at the cocktail party on time and had taken full advantage of the refreshments. He greeted me and told me he was delighted that I was coming to the banquet. He then detailed that he had followed my career over the years and was very proud of my accomplishments. I thanked him.

He next recalled when I was first elected to the Legislature and that he rejoiced in that achievement. Again I thanked him. He further recalled when I was elected Speaker of the House of Representatives and that he was mighty happy about this also. I repeated my thanks. He then revealed his delight upon learning that I had been elected circuit judge. Once more I thanked him.

Expanding his chain of commendations and pride in me, he emphasized, "I like to see my friends get promotions and one of these days I would like to see you on the Grand Jury."

I must have smiled or otherwise indicated amusement and he realized he had said something which was not quite what he meant to say, so he clarified: "Ah, Judge, you know what I mean—like what our friend Claude Taylor has got."

Thereafter, every now and then when the Supreme Court would reverse me as a circuit judge, I would say to myself in amusement, "What can you expect from a grand jury?"

## *Copy 'Em Right*

Quince E. Britt came to the House of Representatives as a member for the first time, along with me, in January of 1937.

He was one of the Assembly's most colorful characters. He weighed about 275 pounds but stood only about five feet and four or five inches tall. He represented York County, containing an Indian Reservation which received an annual appropriation from the Legislature. Quince appeared before the Ways and Means Committee, of which I was a member, seeking a larger appropriation for his Indians. He made a terrific and successful plea. While he was there I dubbed him "Chief." He became known as "Chief Britt," and the title followed him as long as he lived. Following his House service, he ran for the Senate and was elected.

He had this stock answer to questions people asked him: "If the people want it, I'm for it. If the people don't want it, old Britt wouldn't have it."

Once, during a campaign rally, he was advocating free textbooks for all elementary grade children in the public schools. He recommended the purchase of printing machines to be placed in the state penitentiary, where prisoners would print the books for free distribution to the children.

During a lull, a spectator yelled to him, "Hey, what about the copyrights?"

As usual, Britt was "on the ball." Without hesitating, he fired back, "By golly, we'll make 'em copy 'em right, and if they don't copy 'em right, we'll make 'em copy 'em all over again."

### *Easy With The Pressure*

Pressure, if used at all, should be gently applied. It works best when camouflaged, like sugar-coating bitter medicine.

One picture is worth a thousand words, say the Chinese. One anecdote is sometimes correspondingly worth a vote in a campaign for Speaker.

In the fall of 1946 I was soliciting the votes of members of the House of Representatives for the office of Speaker. Fred Hiers, with whom I had served prior to the war, had just been re-elected to represent Bamberg County. Our relationship had been such that I expected and hoped that he would promptly commit his vote in my favor.

I went to his office in Bamberg and found that he was not committed to my opponent, but he was cool to my candidacy. The reason soon surfaced; it developed that newly-elected Governor Strom Thurmond had visited in Bamberg and pressured Fred to vote for me. It was no secret that Thurmond favored my candidacy. He had pressed Fred too hard. He let me know that he wasn't committing his vote because I was so closely associated with the new Governor-elect.

Realizing that this was not the time to push the issue, I tactfully dropped the discussion and suggested to Fred that we eat lunch together and then I would return to Spartanburg. We ate, and I walked back to his office with him. We were standing at the foot of the stairs when I remarked, "Fred, you know your not being for me because of my association with Strom Thurmond reminds me of a story I once heard." I proceeded to relate it:

"There was a man who owned sixteen pigs. He died without leaving a will, and his two sons agreed to divide up the pigs. The first said to the other, 'I will divide them into two groups of eight each; you can have your pick and I will take what's left.'

"The first son knew that his brother had a special pet among the pigs, so he placed the pet with the seven skinniest pigs. Then he grouped the eight fattest pigs in one bunch.

"When it came time for the second son to choose, he put his arm around his pet pig and said, 'I sure do love you, honey, but I can't stomach that crowd you are affiliated with.'

Fred got the point; he laughed heartily and suggested that we return to his office and talk about the election again.

I gladly complied, and before I left his office he had promised to vote for me, and when they called the roll at election time he did just that.

## *"Wired" For Constitutionality*

Fred Hiers was a barber at Ola. He studied law at night, stood the Bar and was admitted to practice. Soon thereafter he was elected as a member of the House of Representatives and brought with him to the meetings a good sense of humor. This quality served him well one day when he was speaking in behalf of the passage of a new law. All members, when they are sworn in, must promise to uphold the Constitution. This means that no legislator must vote for any bill he believes to be unconstitutional. Each member must make this determination for himself as relates to each particular piece of legislation.

As Fred was advocating the passage of the bill, a fellow legislator arose and asked him, "Do you think this bill is constitutional?"

Fred drawled out loud and clear, "Well, I'm not positive about that, and I'm not sure anyone else knows. Up there in Washington they have nine men on the Supreme Court. One day they say something is constitutional, five to four; next day they say it's unconstitutional, four to five." He paused to let this sink in and then added, "It just depends on which crowd sends in the most telegrams."

## *Wind Versus Waves*

In 1954, while I was holding court in Conway, Hurricane Hazel hit the Myrtle Beach area with devastating force. The storm lasted through the night and into the early morning.

After recessing the court, the sheriff and I went out to the beach to see how much damage had been done. We found many houses had been washed out into the ocean and had completely disappeared. Others were total wrecks and sort of shredded, as if they had been run through a giant food chopper. Many other homes were swept back into the marshlands, while others were only washed off their foundations, and some onto an adjoining lot.

One fellow said the hurricane was the best thing that had ever happened to him. He pointed out that "before the hurricane all I had was a vacant lot. Now, I have a six-room bungalow and a new Oldsmobile sitting in my yard."

The chaos created such a dramatic disaster scene that I had Mrs. Littlejohn come down from Spartanburg the following weekend, and we went to the beach to observe together. United States Senator Olin D. Johnston was also there, looking over the devastated area.

Most of the property owners had insurance. Disputes had already arisen between the insurance companies and the owners of the buildings. The burning question was: Did the insurance policy cover the loss? Insurance policies issued on beach property ( and most other ) specifically excluded water damage but included wind damage. So the factual disputes arose because the property owners claimed the wind in the hurricane caused the damage, while the insurance companies claimed that the waves, or water, caused the damage. Many lawsuits resulted; most of them were settled on a fifty per cent basis.

Senator Johnston had served as Governor on two occasions and had served in the Senate for ten years. He was one of the most sagacious vote-getters I have ever known. He had an unusual knack of detecting what was bothering people, and knew exactly what to say to ingratiate himself and bring in the ballots. Thousands of Myrtle Beach voters had millions of dollars dependent upon an answer to the question: Did the wind or the water destroy the property?

After Senator Johnston had viewed the destroyed property, he was interviewed by the Associated Press. His only comment was: "I have looked the situation over to my own satisfaction, and there isn't a shadow of a doubt about it—the wind did the damage."

## *This One Was "Serious"*

Persons in politics feel it a duty to pay their respects at many funerals.

During the early 1940s when I was in the House of Representatives, I attended the funeral of a friend who had died in the Pauline section. The service was held at Philadelphia Baptist Church, and before it began many of us were standing around outside, visiting and talking.

A heart attack had taken my friend. I was chatting with one of his neighbors and commented, "I never knew he was having heart trouble. Had he ever had a heart attack before?"

My friend, speaking very solemnly said, "Yes, he had, but it never was this serious before."

## *"Poor Mouthing" Pays*

When I first ran for the legislature in 1936 I was twenty-three, tall and slender with black hair. Also in the campaign that summer, but running for county solicitor, were Allen Lambright and J. C. Mooneyham, both members of the Spartanburg Bar and both also tall and slender with black hair.

In that year we were at the tail end of the depression. Many people were living hard, and during the campaign a lot of them were attempting to pluck contributions from candidates by working for them at the polls on election day or having their hands out for "gasoline money." These enterprises were treated as a joke among the office seekers. It was not unusual for the same man to work both sides of the street—by accepting money, if he could get it, from opposing candidates.

We were nearing the end of the campaign and heading into a county-wide rally at the courthouse. As I approached the edifice about six-thirty p. m., a fellow from Arcadia pounced upon me with a proposition to help me on election day—for cash, of course. He said he was related to nearly everybody in his precinct, that all of his nearly 400 kinfolks there always sought his advice on how to vote, and he wanted to use his influence in my behalf. There was one catch: he "needed a little gasoline money."

By then I had learned that the only way to get rid of a fellow like that was to "poor mouth" him. If you rejected his offer, he'd go away mad at you. If you expressed any doubt that he actually could help you or called such handouts a waste of money, he'd also be mad at you. But nobody could get mad at you for being poor, so I put on my impoverished act for this man.

Actually, my "poor mouthing" was for real. I was fresh out of law school and campaigning on $100 I had borrowed from my cousin Broadus Littlejohn, so I "poor mouthed" him so completely that when I had finished my sad story he said, "Well, I want you to know I've been helping you already and I'm going to keep on helping you. Everybody I see over there I tell 'em to vote for Lambright."

Somewhat amazed at his candor, I inquired, "Is that really what you have been telling the voters on my behalf?"

He reaffirmed, "Yes, sir. I tell 'em all to vote for Lambright."

"Do you know who you're talking to?" I asked.

He came back with "This is Mr. Lambright, isn't it?"

I spiked him with this strategy: "Why, certainly not. My name is J. C. Mooneyham."

This stopped the would-be huckster cold, and he departed swiftly.

## *Ballot "Brothers"*

In 1936 when I began my first campaign for the House of Representatives, I knew comparatively few people in and around Spartanburg, having spent most of my life up to that time in my native small town of Pacolet.

Near the outset, a friend suggested that I should contact veteran groceryman Broadus Littlejohn, pointing out that he had a multitude of friends and could be a helpful influence if I could enlist his assistance. Accordingly, I went to the store he and Paul Smith operated on Trade Street and solicited his help. Broadus is a distant cousin of mine and has been of tremendous help to me over the years in all of my political endeavors.

As I traveled over the county, more and more people would ask me if I was kin to Mr. Littlejohn. At first I told them we were distantly related, but later when I learned that many of his close friends were agreeing to help me because of this kinship—and as more people mentioned this to me—Broadus and I became closer kinfolks.

After the campaign ended, I told Broadus the longer it lasted, the closer kin he and I became, and if the election had been held two weeks later, we would have been twin brothers.

The names Broadus Littlejohn and Bruce Littlejohn being quite similiar, every now and then I have been mistaken for Broadus. Once, when I was campaigning in Chesnee, where he had a Community Cash Store, I encountered one of his local customers, introduced myself and let it be known that I was running for the Legislature.

This voter beamed and exclaimed, "Oh yes, Mr. Littlejohn, I'm going to vote for you because I always like to trade at your stores."

Not wanting to rock the boat by admitting that I was a lawyer and not a merchant, I settled with, "That's mighty fine. Tell all your friends to help you elect me, and when I get to Columbia I'll do the best I can for you."

## *The Sheriff Shifted*

In 1968 my close friend Charlie Alverson was elected sheriff of Spartanburg County.

He had been a state highway patrolman, a county policeman and had worked with South Carolina Law Enforcement Division for several years. He resigned from the latter organization, usually called SLED, to make the race. I concocted this story on Charlie to tell after the election and have repeated it at several banquets.

When Charlie was with SLED, his superior officer, Chief Pete Strom, told me that if I ever needed to go anywhere on some sort of semi-official mission and didn't have covering expense money, I could call upon Charlie to take me. Accordingly, when I needed to go to Columbia to make a talk to the Magistrates Association, I called Charlie and told him I thought we had better go to Columbia.

He responded, "That's fine, Judge. Where will you be and when can I pick you up?"

Later I needed to go to Sumter to address some F.B.I. School graduates, so I called Charlie and told him we should go to Sumter.

He said, "Judge, that's fine. Where will you be and when can I pick you up?"

Once I needed to go to Florence, so I called Charlie and told him we should go to Florence. Again he answered, "That's fine, Judge. Where will you be and when can I pick you up?"

Then Charlie got elected sheriff.

Soon thereafter, I telephoned him, "Charlie, I believe we ought to go to Anderson today."

He replied, "That's fine, boy. I'll be at home. When are you going to pick me up?"

## *Friendship Fabricated*

Lawyers and politicians are usually sociable folks. They have a habit of referring to their adversary as "my friend" or sometimes "my good friend."

In 1948 I was running for re-election to the House of Representatives and had considerable difficulty with an opponent, F. M. Easterlin. He headed the South Carolina Old Age Pension Association and disliked my candidacy because I had refused to allow him to designate one member of the Free Conference Committee on the State Appropriations Bill when I was Speaker of the House in the spring of 1948. At every speaking rally he assaulted another candidate—Tom Butler—and me. Near the end of the campaign he made a radio speech against both of us.

After the election, a friend at Pacolet told me he had voted for Mr. Easterlin because of the latter's friendship with me. I asked him how he figured it that way and he related, "One day I was eating lunch and the radio was on. I wasn't particularly listening, but I did cock my ear just enough to hear Mr. Easterlin refer to you as 'my good friend,' so I decided to go ahead and vote for him."

## *Chicken Feed For The Judge*

J. William ( Bill ) Davenport was elected Spartanburg County's Probate Judge in 1942. As preparation of this book was being completed in early 1974, he continued to serve and without ever being opposed, as I recall.

Several years ago the people of Chesnee began their custom of serving a free supper to all candidates who assembled there for each election year's speaking rally. These hospitable folks have also invited others to enjoy the excellent food, fellowship and speaking, and so while I was a resident circuit judge in Spartanburg I was invited. Judge Davenport and I went together. Supper was served buffet style.

As we walked along the chow line, Bill was chatting with the womenfolk who were serving and also doing some campaigning, although as usual he was unopposed for re-election. When we reached the lady who was serving up the fried chicken, Bill really turned on the charm. "Lady, it's mighty nice of you folks to fix this supper for us. My name is Bill Davenport. I'm the probate judge. I'm the one who can marry you up." She smiled, selected the biggest piece of chicken on the stack and placed it on Bill's plate.

My turn was next. I greeted her, "Lady, I'm Bruce Littlejohn. I'm the circuit judge. I'm not the one who can marry you up. I'm the one who can turn you loose."

She expressed her delight at our presence, rechecked the chicken, located two large pieces and deposited them on my plate. Her generosity telegraphed a message. First, I knew she was married; secondly, I figured it was entirely possible that she was thinking about trying to get loose from her husband.

## *Service At The Top*

Mrs. Davenport was with us. After we were seated, she looked around, saw a handsome fellow she thought was assisting with serving and called to him, "I wish you would bring me some iced tea."

He promptly and courteously complied and moved on for handshaking. Just about then Mrs. Davenport embarrassedly learned that her "waiter" was Daniel R. McLeod, South Carolina attorney general for several years and out campaigning for re-election.

## *Every Little Bit Helps*

When I was a member of the House of Representatives, just about everybody who talked to me about taxes complained that they were too high. I did encounter at least one exception, a man named Phillips.

He told me, "Bruce, when the Legislature meets, it may be that you will have to raise taxes. If you do, I want you to know that I think it's all right. We've got to have good roads, good schools and good police protection."

At first I didn't ask him how much taxes he was paying, thinking that this would be too personal. Later, I inquired, "Mr. Phillips, how much tax did you pay last year?"

He didn't mind telling me at all.

"I paid $2.37," he disclosed, "but I know that we have got to have good roads, good schools and good police protection, and I don't care if you raise them up as high as five dollars."

## *Ain't No Telling*

The clientele of the Piedmont Cafe, on Magnolia Street and near the courthouse in Spartanburg, provides a well-mixed cross section of people—the rich, the poor, the educated, the semi-illiterate and the illiterate.

I was having lunch there one day in 1960 when the Kennedy and Nixon race for President was under way. Two "rugged-looking" fellows occupied an adjoining table and began talking about the election. Their conversation interested me.

"I'm going to vote for Kennedy," one of them declared.

"Why are you going to do that?" his companion asked.

His friend replied, "Well, Kennedy is rich already; he don't have to steal nothing to stay there. Ain't no telling what that other fellow might take."

## *Ask And Ye Shall Receive*

Billy McGarity of Columbia was among my most loyal supporters in the Autumn 1946 Speaker of the House race. He wasn't a lawyer, but he should have been.

At that time he was secretary to Governor Ransome Williams of Marion County. Ransome was elected lieutenant governor in 1942 and ascended to the governor's chair in the fall of 1944, when Governor Olin D. Johnston defeated incumbent Cotton Ed Smith for the U. S. Senatorial seat. In the summer of 1946, Ransome ran for a full term as governor and Billy made the campaign with him.

Billy enjoyed relating this true story concerning the campaign:

Ransome, an avowed believer in the sale of legal liquor, got into political trouble because of the liberal view he had taken on the liquor issue in the spring of 1946. A campaign meeting was held at Barnwell. Roger Scott, Strom Thurmond, Doctor McLeod and several others had spoken. If I am not mistaken, about eleven candidates for governor were making the race.

The time came for Ransome to speak. Some of the candidates, the press and the prohibitionists had given him a hard time about his stand on the liquor issue. He felt that the issue was cutting deep and decided that the Barnwell rally was the time to go on the defensive.

Although he was not a polished speaker, he attempted to be eloquent and started off by saying, "They have accused me of this, they have accused me of that, they have accused me of the other." Then he asked, "Why did they do it? What have I done?" He paused, sensed he was getting the audience's attention, and repeated, "What have I done?"

After a long pause, the silence was broken by a man in the audience.

"Not a damned thing!" he shouted. That broke up the meeting as far as Ransome getting any votes was concerned.

Billy reported Ransome was quiet during most of the trip back to Columbia but finally acknowledged, "Billy, I guess I asked for it and he gave it to me, didn't he?"

## *Checking A Vote For Justice*

Members of the Supreme Court are elected at a joint meeting of the House of Representatives and the Senate. In 1943 a vacancy occurred on the court and Claude Taylor, who was practicing law in Spartanburg at the time, decided to run for the vacancy. The vacancy occurred during the summertime and, accordingly, those who were seeking the office started a tour of the state, contacting members of the House and members of the Senate with it in view to get commitments for the election that was to be held in January.

Roger Scott was in the House of Representatives from Dillon County at the time. He lived in a rural area near Lake View in that county. Claude went to his house for the purpose of visiting with him and seeking his support, but when he got to the house there was no one at home. In an effort to let him know that he had been there and to let him know that he was counting on him for his support, Claude wanted to leave a note. He was unable to find a scratch pad and so he ended up by taking a blank check and writing across the back of it, "Roger, I'm sorry to have missed you. Hope to see you soon. I am counting on you in the race for the Supreme Court." Signed, "Claude A. Taylor."

Roger had a terrific sense of humor. He was one of those fellows who could take nearly any situation and make humor of it. If he had elected to be an actor, he would have compared well with people like Jack Benny and Bob Hope.

When Claude and Roger got together the next time, Roger approached him and said, "Claude, I can't support you in the race."

This was pretty much of a shock to Claude, because they had been good friends and he had every reason to believe that Roger would be on his side, so he inquired of Roger, "What's the trouble? Why can't you support me?"

Roger's reply was, "I ain't gonna vote for no lawyer for the Supreme Court what ain't got sense enough to know which side of the check he ought to sign when he is trying to get my vote."

## *Discretionary Dividends*

In 1933, while I was a student at Wofford College, Ray Humphrey, also a student, and I decided that we should talk to some lawyer about the advisability of attending law school. We ended up in the office of Sam N. Burts, who had just recently been admitted to practice. Sam recommended that we go to law school, and over the years I have, in good humor, blamed Sam for getting me into law instead of some other profession.

He has been a good friend and strong political supporter through the years, and he was especially active in my behalf when I sought to be elected circuit judge in 1949.

In addition to being an effective trial lawyer, Sam is gifted with a rare sense of humor. Just after my election to the bench, he came to the office and said, "Now, Bruce, I am not going to stand here and tell you that I was responsible for your election, because you have got sense enough to know that already. As you assume your duties as judge, I will not expect any special favors. If you should decide in my favor in a case when you should not, the Supreme Court would reverse you and it woudn't help me any. If the justice of the case is on my side, I know you are going to be with me anyhow.

"The only thing I am expecting is that you let those discretionary matters fall on my side of the fence."

## *Unresurrected*

Politicians learn early in the game that they have to engage in a lot of small talk. They encounter many people whom they know well, but there are a great many with whom they are not thoroughly acquainted. In order to keep the conversation going, they get into the habit of sometimes repeating little things.

One candidate for sheriff in Spartanburg County about thirty-five years ago had the habit of shaking hands with his constituents, asking, "How're you getting along?" and then following up with, "How's your daddy getting along?"

This particular sheriff attended many funerals. He would stand around outside before entering the church and shake hands with all of the local people and renew acquaintances and friendships. They say he went to Pacolet to attend a funeral on one occasion, walked around among the crowd and said to a young man, "How're you getting along?" Then followed it up with the question, "How's your daddy getting along?"

"I'm doing fine, sheriff", the young man informed him, "but my daddy died last year."

The sheriff apologized profusely and assured him that he was sorry to learn this and that he didn't know how the news had escaped him. Then he went on working the crowd. And finally, without realizing it, he got back around to the same fellow again; but he was working the crowd so rapidly and so nonchalantly that he didn't realize that he was talking to the same man. And so he repeated his question, "How're you getting along?" And again he followed it up with, "How's your daddy?"

This time the man reminded him, "Sheriff, I'm doing fine, and my daddy's still dead."

# OF LAWYERS

## *Skinned—Hide And All*

James P. Mozingo III lived in Darlington, practiced law there for some thirty-five years, and simultaneously served in the state House of Representatives and later the Senate.

He was one of the first lawyers in South Carolina to effectively use demonstrative evidence in presenting personal injury cases. One of his favorite visual aides or "props" was a skeleton. He used it to show the jury which bones were broken.

Once a case brought him to Federal Court in Spartanburg; he and associated attorneys roomed at the Pine Street Motel. They brought the skeleton along and each night would caucus at the motel to line up their strategy for the following day in court. The motel maids knew the lawyers were guests but were not aware that the skeleton was domiciled with them.

One morning while the barristers were breakfasting, a maid entered their quarters to tidy up the premises. Moments after she began her chores, she suddenly stopped and excitedly telephoned the desk clerk:

"Them lawyers done skinned one alive!"

## *"Tailored" By Taylor*

Attorney James P. "Spot" Mozingo III had an enviable reputation for obtaining substantial verdicts for his plaintiff clients in civil cases. Rarely did he represent a client who was being sued.

One of these large verdicts by a Darlington jury was appealed to the State Supreme Court. Justice Claude A. Taylor of Spartanburg wrote the high court opinion, affirming the lower court verdict. Delighted, "Spot" headed for a men's wear store and purchased one of the finest suits of clothes in stock. Proudly wearing the suit, he showed up in the lobby of the old Columbia Hotel where Justice Taylor, Otis Bruce and I and several other friends were assembled.

Joining in our admiration of such splendid apparel, Otis said to the strutting attorney, " 'Spot', that's a beautiful suit of clothes. Who's your tailor?"

Promptly and without even blinking, "Spot" placed one hand on Justice Taylor's shoulder and answered, "Claude."

## *Poetic Predicament*

Some doctors once had a habit of arranging to be paged at football games. This was an easy way to get a bit of cheap publicity.

For example, there was a time when the announcer would use the loudspeaker for such "alerts" as this: "Dr. Wilson, report to the emergency room at the county hospital immediately." Finally, in order to stop this practice, a system of assigning numbers to doctors was devised. Thereafter, the announcer's calls were something like this, "Doctor number seventy-nine, you are needed at the emergency room."

One of my lawyer friends and I were chatting one day, and I suggested that the legal profession possibly could work themselves into this announcement publicity too. He liked the idea and suggested this loud speaker system sample:

> Lawyer number 222:
> Your client is in jail;
> Bring bail,
> Without fail.

## *Probatively Qualified*

Many old cases in the law books ended up with new trials granted because of minor infractions of the rules of evidence. I think there formerly was a tendency to be more technical about evidence. Many of the old cases contain rulings which would not be made in modern day courts. One of the things that always plagues attorneys is the hearsay rule, and I might add that this is one of the most misunderstood rules known to the bench and bar.

At the end of World War II, I was assigned to the Philippines as a member of the legal staff named under General Douglas MacArthur to prosecute Japanese war criminals. I found that MacArthur, as commanding authority of that area, had set up rules of evidence for conducting the trials. He had eliminated all the technicalities. His entire directive relative to admissibility of evidence was contained on two mimeographed sheets. Among other things, he said that hearsay evidence need not be excluded and could be admitted for its probative value.

Later, when Captain Arnold Fine and I were prosecuting Colonel Nagahama, charged with committing an atrocity, a witness was asked, "As a result of what you have been told, what did you conclude?" Now, if ever there was an improper question under our American rules of evidence, this was it.

Immediately the defense attorney arose at his table, raised both hands and in effect hollered bloody murder, as he objected on all the grounds known to evidence.

When he finally settled down and concluded voicing his protests, Colonel Sepple, presiding officer or president of the commission, gazed upward as though searching for inspiration and a proper ruling and then, after a long silence, told the defense attorney, "Well, we will let it in for its probative value."

## *Those Stampeding Texans*

About 1969 or perhaps 1970, while Jim Brakfield was coach at Wofford College, the football team had an extraordinarily fine year. Actually, the squad's glory extended over more than a year. They won some twenty or twenty-two games in a row. As a result of their winning streak, they ended up playing a Texas team on New Year's Day. The Texans had an outstanding record also.

The game was scheduled in Spartanburg, but the Wofford stadium being too small for the expected large crowd, it was moved to the Furman University stadium in Greenville.

Those Texans were big men. A lot of them weighed 250 pounds and were more than six feet tall. They literally mopped up the field with the Wofford boys. The score ended about forty-eight to six in favor of Texas.

Lawyers have an unusual and sometimes clever way of expressing themselves. After the game was over, I asked an attorney friend what he thought about the Texas team.

"Judge," he said, "I think those Texas boys charge like an elephant, eat like a horse, run like a rabbit and think like a fox—and see their veterinarian twice a year."

## *A Dream "Come True"*

When my daughter Inell was married in the spring of 1970, a good lawyer friend of mine from Charleston sent her and her husband Dan L. Allen III, a gift. We were not able to determine exactly what it was, although it obviously was a nice present—but one that you ordinarily don't see in stores and gift shops.

Inell knew that in sending a thank you note it was proper for her to state the name of the object she had received, but she was "stumped" concerning identification and asked me to help her out.

I suggested, "Inell, get your pencil and come in here. I will tell you just how to handle it."

She complied and I advised, "You write him this, say, 'Dear Mr. So-and-so, I have always wanted one and now you have made my dream come true. My father thinks a great deal of you.'"

## *Wrath Can Be Wasteful*

As a circuit judge I often spent an entire day or several days trying cases because lawyers on the opposing sides stubbornly declined to settle their litigation. It's just human nature, I suppose, that sometimes attorneys do not like to soften toward opposing lawyers with whom they do not get along. Sometimes they sort of punish each other by prolonging a proceeding.

Occasionally when they made the going rough for each other, I was reminded of an incident that happened in Pacolet back in the 1920s.

A man named L. H. Barnett operated a garage in our small town. A man named Walter McDowell operated a gin about 500 yards away on the same street. Opposite the gin a cotton grower named Charlie Lewis resided. He harvested three or four bales every fall. Lewis and McDowell were not on friendly terms.

At that time it cost only about three dollars to gin a bale of cotton. Lewis didn't want to do any business with McDowell, so one morning he loaded a bale of cotton on a two-horse wagon and headed toward Free's Gin, located five miles away. As he drove past the garage, Barnett realized that Lewis had bypassed McDowell's gin. This prompted him to observe:

"Ain't it inconvenient to be mad at people?"

## *Unimpeachable Credibility*

When arguing a case to the jury, it isn't often that a lawyer can determine just what the jurors are thinking. Normally a juror listens quietly and somewhat reverently.

Sam R. Watt, solicitor of the Seventh Judicial Circuit from 1930 until 1952, was a very capable and effective prosecutor. In Gaffney, Sam was prosecuting a case in which the guilt or innocence of the accused hinged upon the testimony of a Mr. Brown, who was a highly respected citizen of the community.

Defense counsel was painfully aware of the fact that Mr. Brown's testimony was the key to the verdict. He had to discredit the testimony of this witness or lose the case. He therefore argued that the testimony of Mr. Brown was not credible and should accordingly be disbelieved.

When the time came for the solicitor to make his closing argument for conviction, he faced the jurors and effectively argued: "The people of this community have known Mr. Brown all of his life. You know that he is a man of unimpeachable character and integrity. I would like to ask you, as reasonable jurors, do you believe that he would come into this court and tell a lie?"

Spontaneously, one of the jurors spoke out, "Why, certainly not!"

The solicitor smelled victory and closed the argument. The jury retired and promptly convicted the defendant.

## *Burned By Backfire*

Questions asked on cross-examination sometimes backfire.

Solicitor Sam Watt was prosecuting a defendant for grand larceny in the court of general sessions. The defendant produced a witness whose testimony, if believed, greatly weakened the State's case and minimized the possibility of conviction.

The solicitor knew that he had to break down this witness' testimony or possibly lose the case. In cross-examining the troublesome witness, he used the hammer-and-tongs method. Repeatedly he attempted to get him to admit that he was mistaken. He endeavored to induce him to change his testimony, but the witness adhered closely to his original version of what had taken place.

Finally, in desperation, the solicitor asked the witness, "Who have you been talking to about this case?"

The witness responded, "No one."

Still striving to score for the State, the solicitor asked, "Hasn't someone attempted to get you to tell a lie in this case?"

The witness harpooned, "Nobody but you."

## *Take And Give*

Russell McGowan of Charleston was a highly-skilled trial lawyer and knew many tricks of the trade.

Once in Charleston he represented a client who was suing a railroad company for injuries allegedly received at a grade crossing. During the trial he struck a snag. A railroad employee had testified abundantly and precisely about the collision, but when McGowan tackled him during cross examination, most of his answers were vague—"I don't remember," "I can't recall," or "I don't know." Exasperated, McGowan let him leave the witness stand and return to his seat. The moment he was seated, the attorney recalled him to the stand.

On this second round, McGowan challenged the wily witness, "Tell this jury why it is that when the railroad company's lawyer asks you questions you know all the answers but when I ask you questions you don't know anything."

The witness countered, "The railroad company lawyer, he knows how to ask questions just right."

* * *

Later, during the attorneys' argument, the railroad lawyer admonished the jury not to return a "loaded" verdict. He also reminded the panel that sometimes a juror who was especially favorable to the plaintiff would suggest that all twelve jot down a figure, divide it by twelve and let that be the amount of damages awarded. Next he pointed out that someone who was very favorable to the plaintiff would build up the figure so high that it would amount to a substantial verdict, even when divided by twelve. Further, he reasoned, "I realize that jury service is to some extent an exhange of views. There is in jury service an element of give and take."

McGowan in arguing told the jury, "I want to agree with counsel for the railroad company. Jury service is a matter of give and take. And all I'm asking you to do is take it from the railroad company and give it to my client."

The jury did just that.

## *Ouch!*

In the trial of cases a good lawyer instinctively tends to object to questions asked by an adversary lawyer if the suspected answer is going to damage his side of the case. There is involved a sort of reflex objection. Sometimes the objection is totally unwarranted and the attorney is hard put to state the ground of his objection.

On one occasion, the plaintiff's lawyer asked a question which obviously would be detrimental to the defendant's case. The defense attorney quickly objected.

I could see no ground for the objection and inquired, "On what ground?"

He paused, meditated momentarily, and admitted, "Judge, my objection is, it just hurts too bad."

* * *

On another occasion, an attorney objected to his adversary's question and when asked the grounds of his objection, stated, "It might influence the jury."

The lawyer who had asked the question was frank to admit, "That's why I asked the question. My client sent me here to influence the jury."

* * *

Still another time, a lawyer objected to a question and upon being asked what was the ground of the objection, stated, "It's prejudicial."

I overruled the objection and assured counsel that both sides could put in something prejudicial to the other so long as they stayed within the rules.

During a recess that followed, the lawyer came back in chambers and commented, "Actually, prejudicing the other fellow's case is, I suppose, the name of the game."

## *Almost Shocking*

Prior to the 1960s ( when the Supreme Court of The United States virtually ended capital punishment by granting stays of execution ), quite a few persons were sentenced to and suffered the penalty of death by electrocution.

Joe E. Hines Sr. of the Spartanburg Bar enjoyed a good criminal practice. He likes to tell about one man he defended for murder who got close enough to the electric chair to smell it but never sat in the seat.

Some of the most anxious moments that any lawyer experiences are those spent waiting for the jury to knock on the door and return a verdict. In South Carolina in a murder case, if the jury returned a verdict and said, "guilty of murder with recommendation of mercy," the penalty was an automatic life sentence. If the jury returned a verdict which merely said, "We find the defendant guilty of murder," the automatic sentence was death by electrocution.

In this particular murder case, Mr. Hines was somewhat irritated by the fact that his client had failed prior to the trial to tell him the whole truth about the killing. No lawyer likes to be taken by surprise. The jury had been out for some little time and finally returned to the courtroom where the clerk announced the verdict, which dictated the electric chair. The verdict read, "We find the defendant guilty of murder."

Mr. Hines understood the impact of the verdict completely, but his client, a somewhat ignorant person, did not appreciate what was going on. He grabbed Mr. Hines by the coatsleeve and said, "Mr. Hines, how much time did they give me?"

Mr. Hines, still a bit irritated because his client had not told him the whole truth, turned to him and said, "Damn little."

( By reason of motions for new trials and other legal maneuvers, the penalty was finally changed to life imprisonment. )

# BAR, BENCH AND BYWAYS

## *Terra Firma "Hijacking"*

For many years I have enjoyed attending the Judges Conferences held incident to the American Bar Association's annual conventions. Participating in these assemblies has enabled me to visit such places as Miami, New York, Montreal, Philadelphia, St. Louis, San Francisco and Honolulu.

When we flew to Miami, quite a few planes had been hijacked into Cuba, and hijacking was among conversational topics.

Airline stewardesses are pretty and talented, and the one aboard en route to Miami certainly was qualified in both departments. As she was serving me coffee, I asked her, "Young lady, have you ever been hijacked on a plane?"

Mischievously and sweetly she murmured, "One time—and twice in the back seat of a Ford."

## *Homesick For Hills*

At Camp Lee, Virginia, during World War II, I spent the first sixteen weeks of my training, basic it was, in Company H.

Finally this introductory ordeal ended and we were eating our last meal in the mess hall, when speculation arose concerning where the men at the table would be assigned when they moved out of the company the next day.

With us during the discussion were several men, I recall, including a man named Lieberman, a former C. P. A. from Chicago. Also with us was a young fellow named McCall from South Carolina. McCall was born and reared in the mountains and had never learned to read and write until he entered the Army. At Fort Jackson, while he was waiting to be assigned to a training center, he was sent to the Special Training Battalion where instructors undertook to give a student the equivalent of a fourth-grade education in about six weeks. They taught a man enough to enable him to read signs and be of additional service to the Army.

One of our fellow chow-hounds said, "I hope when I move out of here they send me over to Company K." Mr. Lieberman preferred Company B. Others expressed various new unit choices.

McCall remained quiet until the others had completed sounding off, then he finally spoke up. "When I leave here, I'd like to be transferred to Company SL," he said in his deep Southern drawl.

I had never heard of any Company SL, so I kept quiet, but Lieberman was curious.

"What is this Company SL?" he asked McCall.

"That's Sivilian Life," the homesick GI informed us, and then blushed with amazement at the roar of laughter he produced. He never knew why it was funny.

## *Juvenile Judgments*

My children's impressions and expressions when they were very young never ceased to amaze me.

Here are some samples:

When my daughter Inell was five, a little friend asked her what her daddy did for a living.

"I don't understand it exactly," she replied, "but when you want somebody to sue you, you've got to see him."

* * *

When Inell was about four, she came to Spartanburg County Courthouse to watch me preside over a summer term of court.

When I returned home that night, she confronted me with a question of special importance to her: "Daddy, why do you wear your bathrobe while you're working?"

* * *

Once she brought a very young friend home with her. If I remember correctly, it was little Mary Chapman, who then lived on South Fairview Street near our home.

Now youngsters as well as adults often see "judges" on television, but Inell was proud to present the real article.

"Come in here, Mary," she introduced me. "I want you to meet a real live judge!"

* * *

On another occasion a young friend of my son, Cameron Bruce Jr., then very small, expressed doubt that I was a judge. Cam immediately chose to present visible proof.

"If you don't believe he's a judge," he told his tender-age pal, "just come over to my house and I'll show you his hammer."

## *Curious Offspring*

Lie detecting machines are amazingly accurate, even though results of tests on them are not admissible in court as evidence.

When O. L. Brady Sr. of Spartanburg was Chief of the South Carolina Law Enforcement Division in Columbia, I visited with him in 1958. While I was there he demonstrated his lie detecting equipment and did a test on me.

When I returned home I told the members of my family about the tests and described the workings of the machine. My son Cam, who was about eight years old, appeared to be fascinated by my report.

"While I was there," I revealed, "Chief Brady tried the lie detector on me."

"Daddy," Cam inquired, "did it fit you?"

## *Don't Grin Him Guilty*

Many trial lawyers develop techniques which in time characterize them. Those that work well are rarely if ever dropped. Reuben Long of Conway smiled at jurors while making his closing arguments. He had a broad and infectious grin which jurors warmed to and liked.

Once when he was prosecuting a defendant, Senator James Stevens was defending. Aware of Long's smiling habit, Stevens told the panel during his closing argument, "Now, Mr. Foreman and gentlemen of the jury, sometimes I lose a case. The law of averages says no one lawyer can win them all. I have no complaint if my man is convicted on the evidence, but one thing I want to ask of you is this, don't let Mr. Long grin my man into the penitentiary!"

* * *

Reuben also figured that it was difficult for a lying witness to look straight at the examining lawyer, the jury or the judge. In another case, during cross-examination, he asked a witness a question which if answered truthfully would land the defendant in prison.

The witness hesitated and dropped his head, whereupon Reuben prompted him, "You might just as well go on and tell the truth now. The jury has seen you looking at the floor."

## *Hoeing And Habeas Corpus*

For seventeen years I held a term of criminal court in Union early each May. While thus engaged, I would usually drive to Union from Spartanburg, often stopping at Pacolet and visiting with my parents.

When my father was about ninety-one, I stopped at the house one morning about nine o'clock and found him hoeing vegetables in his garden. He was wearing a safari hat. The sun was well up in the sky and it was getting rather warm.

After we had exchanged greetings, I remarked, "Pop, it's getting pretty hot. Don't you think it's about time you stopped and went to the shade? This is no time of day for you to be out here hoeing in the garden."

He loved his garden and he didn't want any of his children telling him what to do, so he looked at me and reminded me, "Son, you may understand the habeas corpus law and those writs of mandamus, but you don't know anything about gardening. Why don't you just go on down to Union and tend to your business while I tend to my garden?"

I did exactly that.

## *The Train Was On Time*

Soon after World War II, Justice Felix Frankfurter of the United States Supreme Court came to Spartanburg to address the annual convention of the South Carolina Bar Association.

It was a singular event for the town, and many people welcomed him in various ways. Pete Kleitches had a restaurant on Morgan Square, downtown, just across the street from the Cleveland Hotel where the justice made his headquarters. Pete was among those who wanted Justice Frankfurter to know that he was happy about his coming to Spartanburg. On his front window he had a sign painted which read as follows: "Welcome Frankfurter." Just below this greeting, a smaller sign said, "Hot Dogs, 15¢."

Justice Frankfurter made a public address about seven o'clock in the evening at Twitchell Auditorium at Converse College. He spoke for an hour and fifteen minutes on the origin of the common law. Many lawyers said it was the driest speech they had ever heard. Finally, the meeting adjourned.

A banquet was to follow at eight o'clock, but didn't get started until about ten o'clock because the justice talked too long and because people stayed at the bar longer than usual. At ten-thirty p. m. people were still eating.

Clint Graydon was President of the State Bar Association at the time. He arose about ten-thirty and suggested that everyone continue to eat. And then he said, "We had hoped that Justice Frankfurter could remain and make a speech. He will return to Washington on the train, which is on time and leaves Spartanburg in about twenty minutes. Accordingly, he will not be able to address the banquet group."

One of the lawyers, who had suffered through the earlier speech and stayed at the bar too long, audibly declared, "Well, hurrah for the Southern Railroad Company!"

## *Pigeons Come Last*

In 1968 I was highly complimented when Dr. Charles Marsh, then president of Wofford College, telephoned me that my alma mater wished to confer upon me the Doctor of Laws Degree. The degree was honorary, of course, and was to be conferred during the regular commencement program in Spartanburg Memorial Auditorium.

Just prior to the commencement I received by mail a card from one of my good friends. This was a "stock" card of the kind on display at counters which sell birthday and other special occasion cards.

Its front depicted a man in cap and gown holding his diploma, plus this inscription: "People will compliment you and brag on you and pay tribute to you and honor you and build a statue of you."

On the inside, the message concluded with "And when you are gone, pigeons will roost on your head."

## *It Peels Well*

John Byrd Zeigler was county sheriff at Bamberg when I rotated there in the fifties to hold court.

After we had completed the trial of a murder case, he approached the bench and invited me, "Come by my office before you leave. I want to give you a pocketknife." I accepted and was shown a bucketful of knives in his office. "Take your choice," he said.

"Sheriff," I observed, "it is obvious that you have all kinds. Where did you get all these pocketknives?"

He detailed their source dramatically, as follows: "You will recall the defendant we just finished trying. We got a call to come to a restaurant in Denmark, where a hot supper was being held, because trouble was brewing. When our deputies arrived, the killing had already taken place only moments before. People were standing in the door and there was only one exit, so all those inside who had pocketknives began throwing them under tables. We collected the knives, but we couldn't find anybody who admitted owning one of them. I ended up with a bucketful of pocketknives that don't belong to anybody."

I selected one with a long blade, called a fisherman's knife. I have kept it in my desk over the years. Occasionally, when I use it in someone's presence for opening a letter or peeling a peach, I'm asked, "Judge, where did you get that long-bladed knife."

I tell them the knife is a sort of illegitimate creature because nobody will claim it, and I am sort of holding it in escrow in case the real owner should ever show up. He probably never will.

## *Just "One Question"*

In many states the office of coroner has been abolished and the function of that office is carried on by a physician. In South Carolina we still have the office of coroner. The purpose of an inquest, which a coroner conducts, is to determine how a person came to his or her death and to recommend whether one or more persons should be accused and held for grand jury action. It is not unusual for a coroner to round up the first six available citizens, whose qualifications are oftentimes scant.

The coroner in a South Carolina county once empaneled such a jury. One of them had been "bouting with the bottle," but he agreed to serve and was made foreman of the coroner's jury. When the six had heard the testimony and received the coroner's instructions, they were directed to retire and write a verdict. The foreman, who had imbibed too freely, inquired: "Mr. Coroner, let me ask you one question before we go."

The coroner responded, "Yes, Mr. Foreman, what is it you want to know?"

All the foreman wanted to know was this: "Are they suing for personal injuries or asking for property damages?"

## *"Gimme" Golfing*

I recommend that all young lawyers take up golf. It is an excellent diversion, and if one does not play the game he often finds himself with a group of fellows who want to play and is embarrassed because he cannot participate.

I speak with authority, because I kept putting off learning to play until I was fifty-six. I was too busy—or thought I was too busy—to learn, and one excuse is just as bad as the other. Finally I got a set of clubs, and though I can't truly say that I have thoroughly learned the game, I make the rounds with friends and enjoy the fellowship.

And so it came to pass that during the South Carolina Bar Association convention at Myrtle Beach in the spring of 1973 I participated in a golf tournament along with about thirty or forty others. I have admitted already that I was never an expert, but I was willing. The tournament lasted two days and on the second day I played in the third flight. I enjoyed playing with several attorneys, among them my good friend John M. Scott of the Florence County Bar.

As things turned out, nearly everybody who played received a trophy of some sort at the convention's concluding banquet. To my surprise, one was handed to me. I was the first runner-up in the third flight. In accepting the award, I observed that considerable fraud had been involved because the only way I was able to win was that every time my ball got on the green, no matter how far from the hole, John Scott would holler, "Judge, that's a gimme."

Later that night, State Supreme Court Chief Justice Joseph R. Moss who has never played golf, admitted he was puzzled concerning how important or unimportant my trophy was, so he asked, "Bruce, what does first runner-up in the third flight amount to?"

"Joe," I admitted, "that's the equivalent of being chambermaid to a cow."

## *Timber!*

When I observe people putting on airs and attempting to impress others with such things as name-calling, sporting loud clothes and displaying gaudy jewelry, I am sometimes reminded of this incident related to me by a client when I was practicing law.

He had occasion to visit the home of one of his employees. This was back in the late 1940s, when television was first coming to the Southland and possession of a television set was somewhat of a status symbol, at least in the minds of some people.

My client said that when he arrived at the home of his employee, a common laborer, he was surprised to see that three beautiful oak trees had been removed from the front yard. He described them as having been magnificent trees of much value.

Shocked, he asked the homeowner, "Why did you remove those trees? I thought they were very nice."

The man's explanation was to the point.

"The trees had to go," he said. "People couldn't see my television antenna from the road."

## *By The Numbers*

When a defendant charged with crime is under bond and fails to show up in court, he may be tried in his absence after he has been called at the courthouse door three times and fails to answer. In Union there was a bailiff who was very obedient and promptly did whatever the solicitor directed. He called several absent defendants, in keeping with the solicitor's instructions. None answered.

A little later the solicitor wanted Attorney Raymond Flynn, whose office was just across the street, to come into court to try a case. At that time the number of many telephones had only three digits. That of Mr. Flynn was 432. Nearly everybody in and about the court knew Mr. Flynn's number.

The solicitor turned to the bailiff, thinking that the bailiff knew he wanted Mr. Flynn, and said, "Call four-three-two."

The bailiff promptly went to the front door and obediently shouted, "Four-three-two, four-three-two, four-three-two."

Thinking he had carried out his assignment, he dutifully returned to the courtroom and reported to the solicitor, "There was no answer."

## *Promotion Pleases*

Spartanburg Bailiff Homer Genobles, having called an absent defendant three times at the courthouse door as legally required, was called to the witness stand to testify to that fact so that trial of the accused absentee could properly proceed. Assistant Solicitor J. Wright Nash began his questioning of the bailiff with this statement, "I believe, Mr. Genobles, you are Judge Littlejohn's chief attaché in this court."

The bailiff stammered slightly and answered, "Yes, sir."

When he had finished testifying, Mr. Genobles, profoundly impressed by Mr. Nash's definition of his duties, immediately asked Miss Folsom Smith, the court reporter, "What is this thing Mr. Nash says I am in this court?"

"Solicitor Nash said that you are Judge Littlejohn's chief attaché," she informed him.

Immensely pleased, the bailiff shoved a memorandum pad in front of the reporter and requested, "Miss Smith, set that down on paper and give it to me. I'm going to Asheville Saturday, and I want to tell my friends all about it."

## *Solons In Siesta*

For many years the South Carolina Highway Department issued low number license plates to state officials. In some counties, local officers as well as state officials took much pride in possessing these plates. People got impressions, some good, some bad and some erroneous, about what these numbers actually meant.

Once when I was parked on a street in Walhalla, two small boys noticed that my tag number was "F-22" and one remarked, "Ain't but twenty-one in the state more important than he is."

* * *

Again, I was holding court in Laurens when two elderly men passed my car and spotted the plate number, which then was "F-2." One wondered out loud, "Reckon how he gets a number that little?"

His companion figured, "He must have bought it early."

* * *

Another time I was waiting in my car in Spartanburg for my son Cam to come out of a dentist's office, and was passing the time with some newspaper reading, when I glanced at my rear-view mirror and saw a fellow in overalls looking at my license number, "F-2." He peered curiously at the plate, then at me, then at the plate again. Finally, still curious, he came to the side of the car and inquired, "Say, mister, is you Senator Olin D. Johnston or Senator Strom Thurmond?"

I laughed, succumbed to temptation and fibbed, "I don't believe I have ever heard tell of either one of them. What kind of work do they do?"

"They don't do nothing much," he informed me. "Both of them are up there in Washington."

## *Live Ones Preferred*

Over the last 100 years, the South Carolina Supreme Court has accumulated many portraits via presentations.

Most of them portray Chief Justices, but there are a lot of others—with the result that a display or "hanging-space" problem developed a long time ago. When the Court was in the State House, the portraits were hung around the courtroom walls, but when the Court moved into its present new quarters, it was decided to display them in various places outside the courtroom.

The older portraits of Chief Justices and others pictured men with long, flowing beards, and oftentimes luxuriant mustaches. One day I was discussing the portraits with Miss Frances Smith, the affable and able clerk of the court, when we concentrated on the portrait of a last-century notable of the judiciary who was equipped with an enormous beard and a full mustache.

Indicating that particular portrait, I cautiously ventured, "Miss Frances, don't you think I look better than this bewhiskered Chief Justice?"

She should have been a lawyer. "Yes, Justice Littlejohn, I do," she said "As a matter of fact, all the live justices with jurisdiction look better to me than those bearded jurists who have gone on to claim their reward in another world."

* * *

In addition to being Clerk of the Supreme Court, Miss Frances serves as Secretary to the Character and Fitness Committee and Secretary to the Law Examining Board. Many lawyers and law students seek her aid with all sorts of problems, so that she stays on the telephone a great part of the time. One day she seemed particularly busy, and every time I went to her office to procure some records she was talking on the telephone. Finally she hung up, and I told her that when she died I was going to prepare an appropriate tombstone for her.

She wanted to know what the inscription would be. I responded that I thought it would be appropriate to engrave a telephone in the stone and right beneath it inscribe the words, "Her line was busy."

## *No Firsts For Femmes*

When I read and hear about the debate that goes on relative to Women's Liberation or equal rights for the lady folks in this country, I am reminded of an incident which occurred in The Philippines at the end of World War II.

Several of us who were prosecuting Japanese war criminals in Manila were invited to the home of a Filipino family for dinner one evening. About five of us from the Army's JAG Department attended. The family was large. In addition to the parents, there were three or four girls whose ages ranged from about sixteen to twenty-two or twenty-three.

When we entered the dining room, we observed that the lady of the house and her grown daughters were standing against one wall. It didn't appear that they were about to be seated, so Lieutenant Wall, a Texan and member of our group, turned to the head of the house and inquired something to this effect, "Won't the lady folks be seated?"

The host exclaimed, "In America, do you let the lady folks eat with you?"

Wall replied, "Why yes, we do."

The Filipino father stared at him incredulously and asked, "Why?"

Lt. Wall, having a good sense of humor, let the matter drop with, "Frankly, I don't know of any good reason."

* * *

It was not unusual to see an entire family taking a walk on a street or in a park in the Philippines on a Sunday afternoon. It was routine for the man of the house to walk in front, with the lady of the house immediately following him and their children following in single file, like stairsteps.

Thus women in America may not have all the rights they would like to have, but when you compare their rights and privileges with those of women in some of the oriental countries, you must realize that they fare much better here than in the Orient.

## *Woman Slaughter*

In South Carolina, when a prisoner applies for parole, the State Parole Board sends the judge who pronounced sentence a resumé of facts in the case, including the applicant's prison record and a brief outline of the crime involved. The purpose of this is to refresh the trial judge's memory so that he may recommend parole, oppose it or remain neutral.

Several years after I had held a term of court in Charleston, the Board sent such a set of papers to me. They summarized happenings this way: The defendant had been charged with and convicted of killing a woman. Trial testimony stated she was found dead in bed, naked and with a bullet wound through her chest, and that when the body was discovered the defendant had disappeared but was apprehended within one hour.

When police arrested him, all he had to say was, "I didn't know the gun was loaded."

## *Revenue In Reverse*

At a meeting of the South Carolina Bar Association at Myrtle Beach, the bell hop was taking my bags from the automobile to my room. Making conversation on our way up, I asked him, "Do lawyers tip pretty good?"

He smiled and informed me, "Judge, most of 'em do. But every now and then I get one of 'em what don't understand the nature of the transaction, and when I get his bags to his room, he expects me to pay him a fee."

# MAY IT PLEASE THE COURT

## *Truth Stretching*

A close friend in Spartanburg was telling me and several others about an unusual incident he claimed had to do with a married couple he had known earlier in his native Pickens County.

He said they resided in a remote northern section known as "Horse Pasture," where living conditions were primitively rugged. He further related that the husband weighed about 250 pounds and stood six feet, five inches tall, and that his wife was nearly six feet tall and tipped the scales at around 180 pounds.

As his story-spinning enthusiasm and our skepticism mounted, he said an infant born to them weighed sixteen pounds at birth. Sensing that his veracity was very much in doubt because nobody had ever known of an infant making its debut with so much poundage, I decided to come to his rescue and volunteered, "Fellows, that's right. I was holding court in Pickens at the time. The baby weighed sixteen pounds and was in the fourth grade already."

This "corroboration" was too steep for even my friend to swallow, so he suggested, "Judge, wait a minute. These people are going to think we're both lying. I'll tell you what I'll do. I'll knock off five pounds if you'll put him back in the second grade."

## *Swampland "Stolen"*

Land condemnation cases are the dullest litigation a judge has to try.

In recent years all trial judges have had many of them because of increasing public improvements, numerous new roads and the widening of existing roads. They have a standing joke around State Highway Department headquarters in Columbia about landowners testifying that their most valuable land was taken because the Department required a right-of-way. Highwaymen facetiously say that the reason roads have curves is because the engineers attempt to acquire the best land everybody has and if the road went straight they would miss some of the choice and get some that is sorry.

Sumter County contains much worthless, swampy land. Once the Highway Department proposed to cut a four-lane road right through a man's farm. He rejected the compensation offered and took his case before a twelve-man jury. It became my duty to try his case.

The landowner's lawyer told him, "Just tell the jury what the Highway Department did to you by cutting this four-lane road through your farm."

"Lawyer, they just ruint me," the complainant lamented.

"Well, be a little more specific," the attorney coached. "Tell them just how the taking of this land ruined you."

Pinpointing his complaint, the aggrieved farmer accused, "They took some of my best swampland."

## *The "Good 'Uns" Are Best*

During the trial of circuit court cases involving the failure of purchasers to make car, furniture or other installment payments on time, I often recalled an incident Alex McCullough related. I have also observed that most people who buy on installment aren't greatly concerned with the amount of carrying charges or interest or the duration of payments. Their chief interest is "how much are the weekly or monthly payments?"

While Alex was a student at Wofford College, he worked part time at Spartanburg General Hospital to help defray his expenses. One of his jobs was to investigate applicants for charity care at the hospital. This once took him to Mayo to talk with a man whose wife had entered the hospital. The husband contended they were unable to pay.

Alex attempted to determine the man's financial situation by inquiring into his earnings, taxes, rent, car payments and other obligations. Suddenly he saw a magnificent radio standing in a corner of the room. Now in those days, back in the 1930s, it was not unusual for a man to buy a radio much larger than a desk or table model, but this one was both big and splendid—in fact, a piece of furniture and occupying the entire corner.

Admiringly and curiously, Alex observed, "That's a magnificent radio you have. How much did it cost you?"

Proudly, the charity applicant informed him, "It cost $239.95."

Alex told him, "I bought a radio last week for twenty-one-dollars and seventy-five cents. It gets all the stations in this area; I hear pretty music and all the news and everything there is to be heard on radio."

The fine radio fancier was frank but probably sunk his charity pitch.

"Yes, sir, Mr. McCullough," he replied, "I seen them for twenty-one dollars and seventy-five-cents, but they were two dollars a week and this one was two dollars a week, too, so I just told them, 'Give me the good 'un."

## *Bullbat Time*

While traveling over South Carolina as a circuit judge, I often was interested in observing some of the unique expressions people use in various sections.

For example, down in the Pee Dee area—Florence, Marion, Dillon, Horry, Georgetown and surrounding areas—it was not unusual to hear a man respond "six head," "seven head," "eight head," or whatever the correct number might be, when asked, "How many children do you have?" I have never heard this expression in upper South Carolina or over on the Georgia side.

Another expression which has grown up in the state, and especially in and around the legislature and Columbia, is "bullbat time." I've referred to this several times at judges' conferences and other meetings, but I've never found a judge from anywhere outside South Carolina who knew what I was talking about. "Bullbat time" is the same as "time to have a drink" or "time for a cocktail."

Legend has it that a General Assemblyman from Lexington County who enjoyed having a drink brought the expression to the Legislature, where it caught on.

His version of its origin was that back home in his county it was sort of an unwritten law that folks ought to quit working and take a drink along about the time the bullbats (night birds) emerged from the bushes and began circulating. Sometimes when the bats were tardy in leaving their perches for their early evening forays, it was customary to send hired hands into the woods to "beat the bushes" and roust out the bats so the drinking could get started.

Most South Carolinians know what "bullbat time" is all about, but it is strictly a Palmetto State expression.

## *Degree Cost Twelve Dollars And Fifty Cents*

Those who read biographies of the state's Supreme Court justices and circuit judges in the Legislative Manual may think that the one about me contains a mistake.

The biography indicates that I graduated from Wofford College with an A. B. Degree in 1935 and from the University of South Carolina Law School with an LL. B. Degree in 1936. This is correct. At that time Wofford had a rule whereby a student could finish his junior year and enter Law School. After he had completed two years in Law School, Wofford would give him his A. B. Degree, thereby allowing two years in law to substitute for the senior year at Wofford.

I left Wofford in 1933. In 1935, having completed two years in Law School, I wrote the late Dr. Henry Nelson Snyder, President of Wofford at that time, that I desired my diploma but couldn't attend commencement because my Law School exams were in conflict with the date. He replied that if I could come by his office some afternoon about five o'clock, he would present me with my diploma and degree.

Dr. Snyder's office in the Old Main Building adjoined the offices of Dean Mason DuPre and Wofford Treasurer J. K. Davis, who had a reputation of "getting the money"—hard to come by in those Depression days. When I arrived, Doctor Snyder sent for Dean DuPre and we had a graduation ceremony.

As far as I know, I am the only Wofford graduate who can until this day repeat the graduation address delivered at the time his diploma was awarded. Here it is, just as delivered by Doctor Snyder:

"Bruce, by reason of the authority vested in me by the State of South Carolina, upon recommendation of the faculty and with the approval of the Board of Trustees, I hereby confer upon you the degree A. B. This is your diploma. Take it and may God bless you. But do not leave this building until you pay Mr. Davis twelve dollars and a half."

## *Charleston's Uniqueness*

For more than half a century it has been well-known to most South Carolinians and many tourists that Charlestonians deal with the whisky problem in their own way.

Liquor laws are changed for better or for worse; prohibition comes and goes; but the unique ways of what to do with whisky remain virtually the same in Charleston.

I was staying at the Fort Sumter Hotel there while holding a term of court in the late 1950s. Late one afternoon or evening, I entered the dining room and gave a waitress my order for a broiled seafood platter, one of my favorite dishes. After she had written it on her pad, she said, "Sir, it will take a little time to prepare this for you. Would you like to have a cocktail or highball while we are getting it ready?"

I spoke to her in a serious tone, "Young lady, I am a stranger in this town, but somewhere I got the impression that it was unlawful to serve whisky in the manner you have described. Am I mistaken?"

Her reply was just as solemn as my question. She said, "I don't know, mister. I never went to law school."

I told her, "Well, lady, I don't believe I'll order any, but if you find out whether it is legal or not legal, will you let me know?"

She said, "I'll be glad to," and headed for the kitchen to prepare a broiled seafood platter.

## *Experienced In Discipline*

My friends in the maintenance department at Spartanburg County Courthouse enjoyed relating this true incident which involved my parking space.

My father lived until he was ninety-three years of age and drove his car until about ten days before his death.

One week I was holding court in York and he knew this, because I usually drove through Pacolet where he lived to pay him a short visit on the way. One day during that week he drove to the courthouse to transact some business and proceeded to park in the space that was clearly marked for "Judge Littlejohn."

As he got out of his car, one of the maintenance men approached him and said, "Mister, you can't park in that space. It belongs to Judge Littlejohn."

Pop was about ninety at the time. He looked the man squarely in the eye and said, "Mister, I have spanked Judge Littlejohn before, and if he gives you any trouble about me parking in his space, you let me know, because if it becomes necessary, I can spank him again."

He then identified himself, the man relented, and he left his car there and went about his business.

## *Sounding Off For Seneca*

I'll always pleasantly remember Walhalla Bailiff Captain Billy Hunt. I never knew why the lawyers there and others called him "Captain."

He lived two or three miles from the courthouse and took much pride in relating that he walked home and back. Although he was pushing eighty, he had a long stride of about four feet to the average man's three and was tall and slender.

He also was equipped with a strong pair of lungs and a loud voice.

South Carolina court procedure requires that if a person charged with a criminal law violation does not appear in court at the appointed time, in many instances he may be tried in his absence, but only after the bailiff has called him three times at the courthouse door and received no answer.

Of all the bailiffs I have ever worked with, Captain Billy could call the loudest. He had a reputation in and around Walhalla of being able to let the whole town know when a defendant was absent.

On one occasion, the clerk asked him to call Bill Felder, an attorney who resided in Seneca, some seven miles from Walhalla. This resulted in friends inventing this story about Mr. Hunt while I was there. They spread it around the courthouse that when Captain Billy was instructed to alert Mr. Felder to come to court, he walked to the door and called the lawyer's name three times in his usual loud voice. At this point, so the story goes, the clerk told the bailiff, "I meant for you to phone him," whereupon Captain Billy replied, "There's no use to call him on the phone. He just lives over there at Seneca, seven miles away."

## *Greedy Passion*

Rape case trials usually are solemn affairs, but occasionally something humorous happens to relieve the tension.

Here's an example. A woman had a man charged with rape and testified that he forced her to have intercourse with him.

The question of consent was injected on behalf of the defendant, since under the law if she had volunteered herself, there could not have legally been a case of rape. She testified that the defendant had not only forced her to have relations with him without her consent but had also taken her pocketbook.

Cross-examining, the defense attorney cited other testimony that people were in the room next door and if she had screamed or called out an alarm, someone would have come to her rescue.

"Well, I would have given an alarm," she explained, "but I didn't know he was going to take my money."

## *Just Call Me Olin D.*

Throughout the United States and especially in South Carolina and other Southern states, there formerly was a custom of naming newborn children after politicians and office holders.

This practice has virtually vanished. But in holding court throughout the state I would still meet a few Ben Tillmans, some Cole Bleases, quite a number of Franklin D. Roosevelts and a few Olin D.'s, the latter named for the late Olin D. Johnston.

One Saturday morning around 1955, I was researching law in my office in Spartanburg when Attorney Ray Godshall of Gaffney telephoned to ask if he could bring a client over so he could petition the court to settle a minor's personal injury case.

In South Carolina—as in other states, I suppose—a minor's case cannot be settled where personal injuries are involved unless a judge examines the situation and agrees that the proposed settlement is fair.

I invited Ray to bring his client. About an hour later they arrived. She was about forty-five and weighed around 200 pounds and obviously was a lady of little learning. Mr. Godshall told me what had happened to her son, who was about nineteen at the time. He detailed the doctor's bill, hospital charges and elements of the claim in general.

I thanked him and queried the mother: "Now, Mrs. Wilson, do you understand that if I approve this settlement it brings the claim to an end once and for all, so that neither you, your husband nor the boy, nor anyone else in behalf of any of you, can ever get any more money, regardless of what develops in the boy's situation?" She said she so understood.

"Does your husband have the same understanding?" I inquired. "I notice he is not with you today. Have you talked this over with him?"

Candidly, she replied, "Judge, just to tell the truth, I ain't seen him in about fourteen years. Really, we never were exactly married. He wasn't what you might call a technical man." Realizing I had asked the wrong question and having no desire to embarrass her, I changed the subject and inquired, "Are you convinced that the boy is getting along all right and is back to normal again?" She said he was.

Wishing to put her at ease, I said, "I'm glad to hear it. What's his first name?"

"Judge, he named Olin D," she informed me.

Coincidentally, Mr. Godshall was one of Senator Johnston's closest friends, so he interposed, "Judge, if you will count back, you'll see that this boy was born while Senator Johnston was Governor of South Carolina. People all over the state just loved Olin so much they named children for him by the hundreds."

Records show that they did.

## *Plaintiff Winneth The Noneth*

Now and then the foreman of a jury fails to follow the trial judge's instructions, and writes the verdict in an irregular fashion.

In one case I instructed the jury that they could decide in favor of the claimant and write a verdict which would read, "We find for the plaintiff .................................. dollars."

Disregarding my instructions, they wrote a verdict which when read by the clerk, declared, "We find for the plaintiff nothing."

The losing party is required by law to pay the costs of the trial. Facetiously, counsel for the plaintiff argued that the costs should be assessed against the defendant. When I asked him why, he replied, "The plaintiff won the case, but the jury just didn't give him any money."

Down in Georgia in such an instance, lawyers say that the jury gave him the noneth. It is a word I have never heard in South Carolina courts.